Osprey Modelling • 42

Modelling Scale Figures

Mark Bannerman

Consultant editor Robert Oehler • *Series editors* Marcus Cowper and Nikolai Bogdanovic

First published in Great Britain in 2008 by Osprey Publishing
Midland House, West Way, Botley, Oxford OX2 0PH, UK
443 Park Avenue South, New York, NY 10016, USA
E-mail: info@ospreypublishing.com

ISBN 978 184603 238 7

Consultant editor Robert Oehler

Editorial by Ilios Publishing, Oxford, UK (www.iliospublishing.com)
Design by Servis Filmsetting Ltd, Manchester, UK
Typeset in GillSans and Stone Serif
Index by Alison Worthington
Originated by PDQ Digital Media Solutions Ltd.
Printed in China through Bookbuilders

08 09 10 11 12   10 9 8 7 6 5 4 3 2 1

A CIP catalogue record for this book is available from the British Library.

FOR A CATALOGUE OF ALL BOOKS PUBLISHED BY OSPREY MILITARY AND
AVIATION PLEASE CONTACT:

NORTH AMERICA
Osprey Direct, 2427 Bond Street, University Park, IL 60466, USA
E-mail: info@ospreydirectusa.com

ALL OTHER REGIONS
Osprey Direct UK, P.O. Box 140 Wellingborough, Northants, NN8 2FA, UK
E-mail: info@ospreydirect.co.uk

www.ospreypublishing.com

Acknowledgements

My gratitude and deepest appreciation to Shep Paine, Nikolai
Bogdanovic and Marcus Cowper at Ilios Publishing, Paul 'Hawkeye'
Bacon, Arthur 'Run to the Hills' Sekula, Per Olav Lund, Daniel
'You mock me, Sir ?' Munoz, Denis 'Pour Eduard' Allaire,
Le Van Quang (PiliPili), Paul Quek (Miniature Alliance), Jennifer
Haley, Eddy Vandersteen, Greg Gerault, Clarence Harrison,
Garfield Ingram, John Maher, Lee Dobson, Paul Clarke at
Shenandoah, Roger Saunders (Hornet), Luka at Pegaso Models,
Andrea Miniatures, my folks Pat and Bill, my brother Paul
'Aktiengesellschaft!', and last but not least, my very supportive
wife Elizabeth.

The Woodland Trust

Osprey Publishing are supporting the Woodland Trust, the UK's
leading woodland conservation charity, by funding the dedication
of trees.

Contents

Foreword by Shep Paine

Although I have known Mark for many years, I first got to know him when I was invited to attend a model show in Halifax. Mark was my host on that occasion, and, while he was a pretty good modeller, what I really remember was his gracious hospitality during my visit. He was obviously proud of his home town, and I could not have had a better guide to introduce me to it. We have remained in contact since that time.

It's hard to believe, but this year marks my 40th year in the hobby. Since I first started doing figures, I have seen a lot of changes, and a lot of painters come and go. In the early days, the number of good figure painters in North America could be counted on the fingers of one's hands. Today there are virtually dozens of excellent painters in both North America and Europe. If the quality of work has vastly improved, it is interesting to note that the overall number of people painting figures does not seem to have increased much.

Perhaps what is needed is a good basic introduction to the hobby, designed specifically for the person who has never tried it before. Most books (including mine) tend to focus on the needs of intermediate and advanced modellers who need help moving up to the next level. Even in the books that do try to cover the basics, this information is often overshadowed by the bulk of the material that follows it. A modeller who is struggling to find a good basic flesh colour isn't ready to learn about sculpting faces and is often intimidated by a book that tells him how to do that.

So, Mark has set out to write a book specifically for people getting started or dabbling in the hobby. Whatever our level of experience, we all need to crawl before we can walk, and to walk before we can run. A lot seems to have been written about walking and running, but not a lot about crawling. So if you feel you are still at a crawling stage, then this book is for you.

It's time to get out your paints and let Mark guide you through the process step by step. And remember that this is a hobby. How well you do it is not as important as how much enjoyment you derive from it. So don't sweat the small stuff, and have a good time!

Introduction

One of the most common complaints from figure modellers is that they often feel their abilities have reached a plateau – that they've reached a point where they cannot improve further. One of the reasons for this is that modellers typically stick to their comfort zone, and don't try new techniques. As a result, their styles and abilities stagnate. The solution to overcoming this stumbling block is to try new approaches. Trying new techniques is the only means of improving your skills, and will also help to further your personal finishing style.

There are many techniques for modelling and painting figures. Over the years, I have tried almost every one that I have seen or read about, logged the pros and cons of each, compared one to another and determined which I preferred. By and large, the easiest methodologies prevailed. The techniques in this manual are a compilation of those tried, tested and true approaches. I believe these to be the easiest and most user-friendly techniques for the avid figure modeller. As such, this manual was written as a reference guide for enthusiasts who are starting in the hobby, or for those who want to try new techniques and improve their own styles.

The topics in this manual are generic enough to allow you to apply the same techniques to subjects of various scales from many eras. As well, you will find the answers to some of the more common assembly and painting questions.

This manual does not attempt to cover every aspect of this vast hobby, but rather to provide the basis for many aspects of the hobby that are not as well covered in print form. To pack as much information and photographs as possible into this manual, I will not always show figures being assembled or painted from beginning to end. Rather, I will demonstrate specific steps and

A typical resin figure kit. Parts are neatly moulded and detail is very crisp. Some carrier will need to be removed. This is a PiliPili resin musketeer and instructions on assembly and suggested painting guide are very clearly shown.

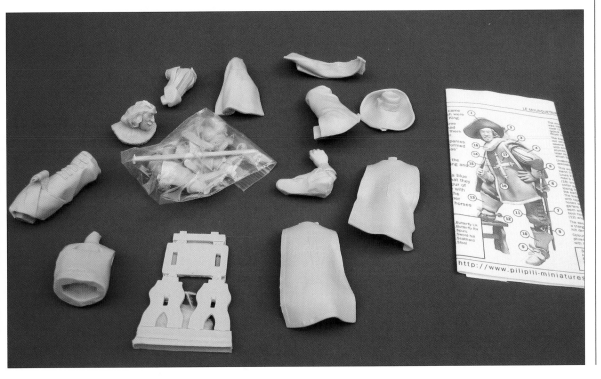

The plastic figure market is huge and offers the largest range of figures that are readily available in all sizes and subjects within very attainable price ranges. The variety of scale and subject is second to none.

techniques to allow the reader to 'get started', as it were, in a challenging or unfamiliar area of the hobby and the reader can then further develop his or her own techniques.

With thousands of figures on the market, it is worth discussing the types available. The most popular, inexpensive and readily available figures are made of injection-moulded plastic. The typical set contains four to eight figures, usually broken down with separate upper torso, arms, heads, helmets and legs. Plastic figures offer ease of assembly, many conversion possibilities and a general consistency of scale among manufacturers. The disadvantage is that plastic figures are not quite as crisp in detail as their more expensive white-metal and resin cousins. Some of the more popular plastic figures include those by Dragon/DML, Tamiya, Tristar and Airfix.

The second most popular choice among figure modellers is resin. These figures are generally superior in detail over plastic, slightly more expensive and involve less assembly work. The disadvantage is the wide variation of size within the same scale among different manufacturers. Popular resin figures can be purchased from Alpine Miniatures, PiliPili Miniatures, Verlinden, Warriors, Hornet/Wolf and Miniature Alliance.

White-metal figures are generally well sculpted and cast, and offer some of the best figures on the market. The disadvantage of white metal is that it is more expensive, not as easily converted as plastic or resin, and the weight of a figure will almost always require a pin drilled up through the heel to allow the figure to stand on its own weight. The price range for a metal figure will be very wide, but the quality is almost guaranteed. Some of the more popular manufacturers of metal figures include Andrea, Romeo, Pegaso and Elite/La Torre.

Scale denotes the size relationship of a model to the real world and is generally expressed as a fraction. A figure or model in 1/24th scale has dimensions that are 24 times smaller than the height, length, width and depth of its real-world counterpart. Another way of writing this is '1:24', or 'one to twenty-four'. This means that one inch on the model equals 24 inches on the real object.

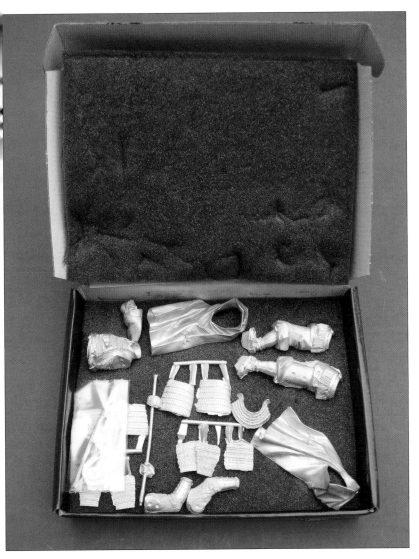

White-metal figure models usually come very well packaged to ensure the contents do not dent or get nicked. White metal is a soft material and could easily be spoilt if it were dropped or knocked about in shipping. This is a 90mm Pegaso Models samurai.

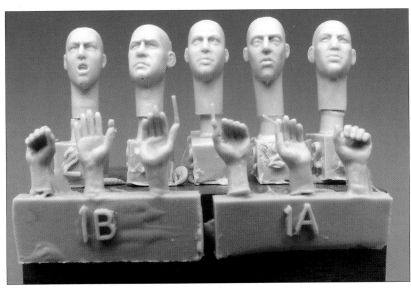

Many after-market accessories are readily available to help the modeller improve the overall appearance of figures. These are some of the excellent after-market resin Hornet heads and hands in 1/35th scale by Roger Saunders.

The newer plastic figures being released offer some very high-quality figures with very good detail. This is a head from one of the Tamiya large-scale 120mm series.

The various figure scales are usually – but not exclusively – measured in millimetres (mm), representing a measurement from the top of the figure base (i.e., the bottom of the figure's foot) to the crown of the head (not to the top of the headdress, if any). There can often be some confusion as to the use of fractions versus millimetres. To simplify this, here is a table showing the approximate equivalencies between fraction, metric and imperial measures.

SCALE TABLE

1/6 = 300mm = 12 inches
1/9 = 200mm = 9 inches
1/12 = 150mm = 6 inches
1/16 = 120 mm = 5 inches
1/24 = 70-75mm = 3 inches
1/32 = 54mm = 2¼ inches
1/35 = 50-51 mm = 2 inches
1/48 = 40mm = 1½ inches
1/72 = 25mm = 1 inch

It should be emphasized that similar scales often vary between manufacturers. For example, miniatures sold as 54mm may actually range between 50mm to 59mm on a ruler. Not all humans are of the same height and therefore, figures of different heights in the same approximate scale can be mixed. On the other hand, too much variation in scale within a single presentation may not look correct to the eye. The key to combining figures of different heights on a single base is to use standard-sized equipment on them.

Selecting a figure is about personal choice. Some look for uniform accuracy, some for clarity and sharpness of surface detail, and some the level of sculpting of the face. Whatever your criteria, it is crucial to examine a figure carefully. Try to look beyond the superbly painted figure on the box art and determine if the figure has the detail, pose and overall appeal you are seeking. Search for a review of the figure on the internet. The most important characteristic in any decision you make about a figure – whether plastic, resin or metal – is to ensure that the figure has a realistic pose and realistic proportions. Fortunately, the human eye is very good at determining the accuracy or inaccuracies of human anatomy. If the pose looks wrong, or un-natural, it probably is.

As you will discover in this manual, painting colourful and different figures can be a nice change of pace from drabs and greys and offers up some new and different challenges. On this in-progress white-metal Pegaso Models 54mm chasseur, the intricate braid work on the tunic provides a different and unique effect.

Assembly and construction

Introduction

The key to successfully executing a figure is to pay as much attention to the construction and surface finish as the painting. There is nothing quite as disappointing as realizing halfway through the paint process that a nasty seam was missed in the preparation stage. Paint will not hide nor camouflage surface blemishes. To avoid this, it is worth taking as much time as necessary to ensure that a figure has no gaps, seams or mould lines. As the old saying goes, 'Measure twice and cut once'.

If the reader is already a modeller (of armour, aircraft, etc.), then you probably already have most of the necessary tools and materials for assembly and construction. For those who are just beginning in this hobby, the up-front investment is quite inexpensive and most of the more specialized tools will last a lifetime with proper care. For the assembly process, the basic tools required are a hobby knife (standard #11 blade), sandpaper (with very fine grit such as #300), glues (liquid, epoxy glue and cyanoacrylate or 'superglue'), putty or filler (such as Squadron Green putty), and nail clippers or small scissors.

Your workplace is equally as important as your tools. I use a small desk with very limited space, but I have the added advantage of being located directly under a window. A natural light source is a huge benefit, especially in the painting process, because natural light provides true colour tones, whereas fluorescent and incandescent light will often alter the overall appearance of

A few tools and materials used for assembling and constructing figures. Toothpicks are ideal for mixing glues and paints. Metal files work well to remove surface blemishes on resin and white-metal figures. I also use blunt dental instruments for removing hard-to-reach seam lines such as inside legs and inside small folds.

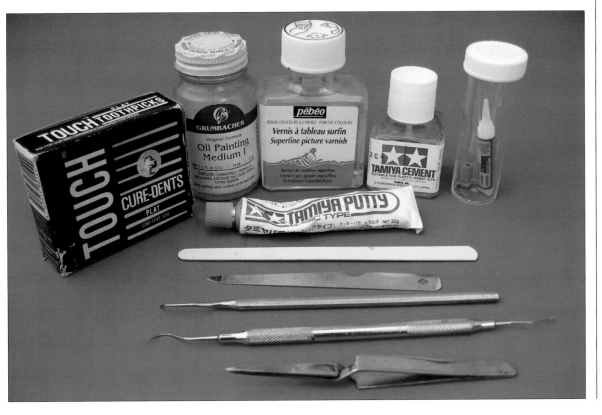

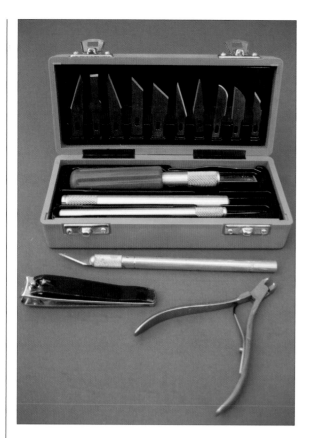

All of my cutting tools are contained in this box. Various types of blades for different tasks – although a regular # 11 blade (attached to the scalpel) will do all of the jobs.

paint tones. If natural light is not available, I recommend the purchase of a high-intensity light that replicates natural light as closely as possible.

The first step in the construction process is to examine the parts of the figure carefully and with a very critical eye – even while the parts are still attached to the parts trees. Plastic parts can be snipped off the sprue with a pair of fingernail clippers. Excess flash or the small plastic nodes should be removed with a sharp hobby knife or sandpaper. Small rough spots can be scraped off with the edge of a hobby blade and smoothed over with sanding. Different-shaped metal files work well for removing seams on resin and metal figures, but are less practical on plastic figures because the rubbing motion tends to quickly gunk up the files. For larger unwanted protruding plastic bits or resin pour plugs, a small jeweller's saw or a saw blade attached to your hobby knife will work well. I frequently use a Dremel power tool with a fine sanding disc to remove excess resin and metal pour plugs, as this usually leaves a fine smooth finish. Make sure you wear a respirator when sanding resin or metal, and work in a well-ventilated area. I don't use a Dremel sander on plastic, because the speed of the sander usually melts the plastic and leaves nasty rough surfaces.

It should be noted that some modellers prefer to paint parts while still on the sprues. This does have the advantage of allowing you to hold the sprue edges. However, there are also several disadvantages. The biggest disadvantage is that once the parts are painted and removed from the sprues, the modeller will have to remove the connector plugs, which will leave unpainted areas. As well, the connector areas will require some sanding, which will ruin any painted area around the connector plug. For these reasons, I strongly recommend you assemble as much of the figure as possible before contemplating the painting process.

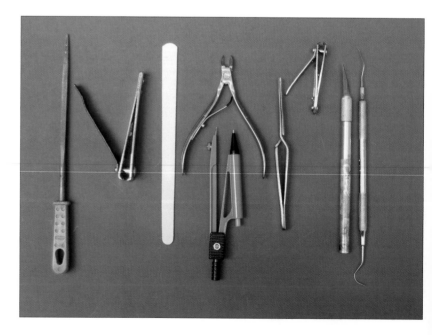

Emery boards work well to file plastic figures, and the two different-sized clippers are handy for cutting larger parts. I usually use the larger nail clippers for big attachment plugs while the smaller ones are used to remove small nibs. I also use an inexpensive compass for measuring details to ensure accuracy, particularly in determining lengths such as rifle straps and belting.

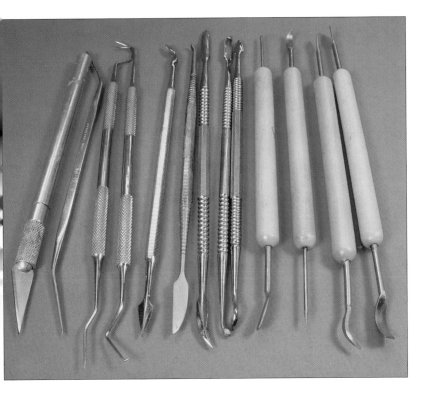

A collection of various tools primarily for conversion, sculpting and scratch-building. One does not need all of these tools but this provides an idea of the various tools that could be used.

Once all of the flash and excess nubs are removed on resin or plastic figures, I apply liquid glue to all areas that were scraped or sanded to help smooth out the areas. For metal figures, smoothing out the surface usually takes various grits of sandpaper. Once all of the surface blemishes are removed, cleaned up and smoothed over, the next step is dry-fitting the parts. Dry-fitting pieces together without gluing allows you to make any necessary adjustments. There is never a guarantee that parts will fit perfectly out of the box; therefore, dry-fitting a figure using a product such as Blu-Tack or another temporary adhesive is very helpful to see how the figure will appear when it is assembled. If the

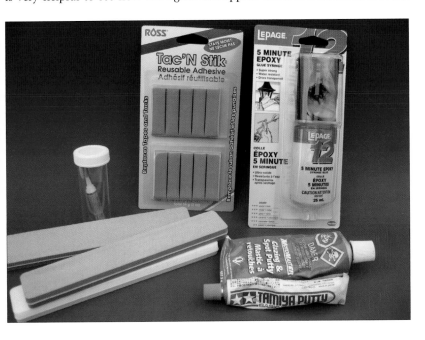

A few sanding sticks, various putties, glues and Blu-Tack adhesive for dry-fitting parts to a figure.

It is worth laying out all of the parts to ensure the kit is complete, and to help determine the approach for cleaning up each part.

Working with figures does not necessarily require the modeller to exclusively use resin or plastic. Copper and brass wire can be very useful, as Per Olav shows us on this conversion piece.

parts do not fit well, this would be the time to begin filing, sanding and tailoring these so that they will fit neat and flush.

To cement plastic figures, liquid glues such as Testors or Tamiya work very well, and have the advantage of allowing the modeller to fiddle a bit before the glue hardens. For resin figures, you should either use cyanoacrylate ('superglue') or epoxy glue, as this provides for a very strong bond between parts. For white metal, I strongly recommend using five-minute epoxy glue. For multimedia figures or conversions, any combination of materials should be bonded with epoxy glue for the heavier parts and cyanoacrylate glue for smaller parts. When attaching parts, only apply glue to one of the joints being attached, not both. In gluing a figure together, keep the head, weapons and all belt accessories unattached until after the main body of the figure has been painted.

As an aside, make every attempt to ensure that the glue sets the first time. Fresh glue added to dry glue does not generally provide a strong bond, so if you make an error, allow the glue to dry thoroughly, then sand it off or scrape it off with a hobby knife and repeat the process. After the figure has been glued, you might note small gaps and cracks – particularly around the joints between the arm and shoulder seams, as well as between the upper and lower torso. These small gaps should be filled with putty. Generally, putty will shrink when dry, so ensure you build up a little ridge along the fill lines so that it can be sanded flush afterwards. To smooth putty when it is wet, use your finger dipped in rubbing alcohol. When thoroughly dry, sand carefully with fine sandpaper until flush. One should allow putty to dry for 24 hours before sanding and filing. If any further gaps or uneven spaces remain, fill them again and allow another 24 hours for drying.

The key is to ensure that a figure has no surface blemishes before painting starts. Be critical and take the time to be certain that the surface and joints are perfect.

Building 'out-of-box'

This Airfix 1/32nd Multi-Pose 'Eight Army' figure has been built out-of-box. The term 'out-of-box' (commonly abbreviated as OOB) refers to only using the parts supplied in the kit box. Adding small additions such as straps and rifle slings not included in the box would only be considered to be correcting the figure and therefore would still be considered OOB.

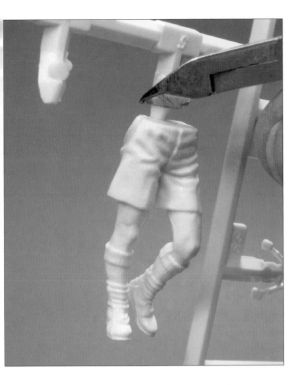

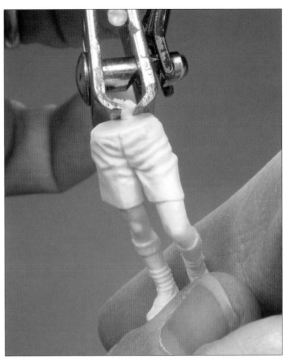

The pieces are cut from the parts tree using a pair of nail clippers. Note that I have cut the connector at the midpoint and not where the connector meets the part.

The connector plug is further removed from the part with a smaller set of nail clippers.

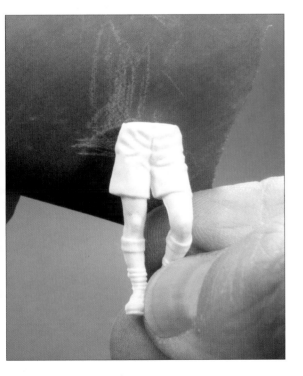

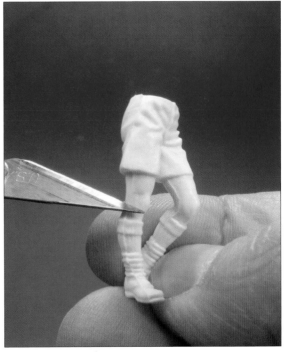

The area is then sanded with light grit paper to eliminate the small blemish and excess plastic.

Seams and flash (you can see a seam running along the side of the left leg) are removed with a scalpel blade in a back and forth scraping motion – not in a slicing or cutting motion.

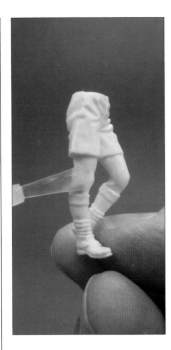

ABOVE Liberal amounts of Tamiya liquid glue are applied to the sanded areas to smooth out the gritty surface that was sanded. A few light applications of gloss coat can also help further smooth out any rough areas once the glue has dried.

ABOVE The main parts of the figure are dry-fitted using Blu-Tack or similar type of adhesive putty to help bring the figure together visually without committing to glue immediately.

A simple conversion project

This 1/35th-scale figure has been cleaned up and partially glued together using various commercially available parts such as plastic injection arms (DML), resin torso (Warriors), resin footwear (Verlinden) and a resin head (Hornet) with a plastic helmet (DML). This figure would be considered a 'simple conversion' using a combination of parts from various kits.

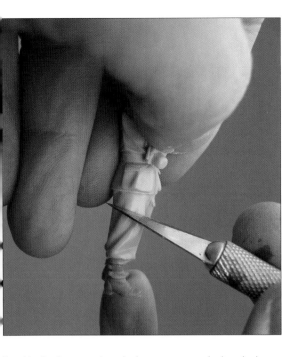

For this simple conversion, the boots were attached to the lower leg with superglue. Here I am removing a fine seam line along the outer trousers.

The figure has been cleaned up. Note the rough areas on the inner thigh. These will be addressed with liquid glue applied directly to the rough areas to help smooth out the surface.

After dry-fitting all of the parts with Blu-Tack adhesive and cleaning up small blemishes, I glued the arms to the upper torso with a small amount of superglue. The head is only temporarily attached with Blu-Tack as this will be easier to paint separately from the body.

I carefully wedged small amounts of automotive putty into all of the gaps with the tip of a blunt hobby knife. I followed this by applying liquid glue to the joints to smooth out the putty. Once the putty has fully cured, sandpaper was lightly rubbed over excess putty to bring the joints to a smooth finish.

The figure is assembled. The key before moving on to the next step of painting the figure is to carefully analyse the figure to ensure it looks correct. Try to imagine how it would look with paint and whether the stance and pose look realistic.

A last-minute alteration. I decided to change the hands, as I felt these were 'soft' and not expressive enough. I cut the plastic ones off with nail clippers and drilled a hole into the arms, then inserted after-market Hornet resin hands.

Major conversions

A major conversion is one step further than the simple conversion. Typically, a major conversion takes on the form of altering and changing the overall appearance of a figure by using the 'skeleton' from an existing figure and making changes using putties and sometimes wiring. This is fast becoming a popular form of the hobby because modellers are looking for a specific pose in a precise size for a particular scene or diorama.

Complete conversions of figures require several new skills and it is important to have a relatively good grasp of the basics of the proportions of the human body. Once a pose or stance has been determined, the modeller works the putty onto the figure in layers to transform the figure's appearance. Putties specifically made for this purpose include Duro, A & B Putty and Milliput. In this example, Per Olav Lund has transformed a Hornet 1/35th-scale rendition of Hornet's 1/35th-scale Montgomery into a Norwegian civilian using Magic Sculp and Duro putty. To make the putty more workable, Per uses baby oil to help smooth out the surface.

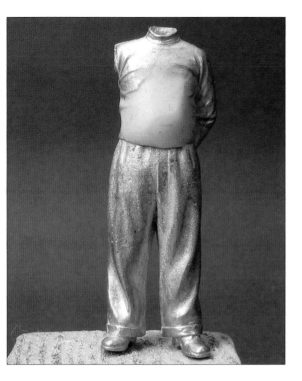

To alter the figure's body from the original, a bigger belly was made from Magic Sculp.

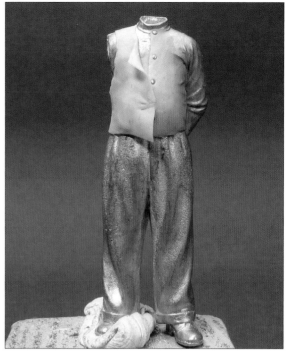

Buttons were made with a punch and die set, and lead foil was attached to the shirt. A very thin sheet of Magic Sculp was rolled out and affixed to the chest to represent the figure's vest.

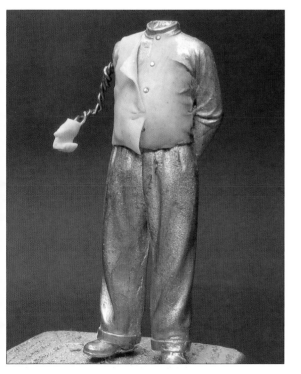

A wire armature was used as a base for the right arm, while the grasping hand is from the Hornet range of after-market accessories.

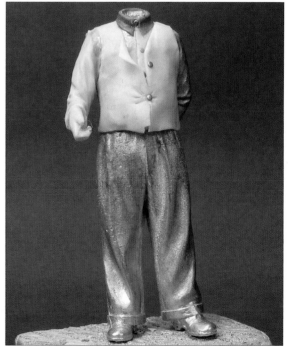

The right arm has been covered using Magic Sculp and carefully worked with blunt tools to denote the natural folds. The dark green shirt collar was made with Duro epoxy putty.

The head is from the Hornet range and personal touches were added to the face to give more character. The original ears were sliced off and positioned at a new angle, some sideburns were added using Duro epoxy putty and the tea kettle was made from scratch using plastic rods. The bottle and mug came from the spares box.

The finished figure. Note the transformation from the original Hornet offering to a unique piece. The transformation makes the new figure a one-of-a-kind.

The converted figure placed on a diorama, alongside other heavily converted figures.

Working with metal figures

The construction of metal figures requires the same care and attention as any other medium. On this 54mm Andrea knight, all of the parts were laid out for careful review. Metal figures will almost always require a pin or post to be drilled into the heel of a figure. The sheer weight of a metal figure will necessitate added support once it is placed on a base. Glue on its own will simply not provide the support.

RIGHT The plug on the underside of the figure's foot was cut off with large nail clippers. Ensure you wear protective eyewear when working with metal figures.

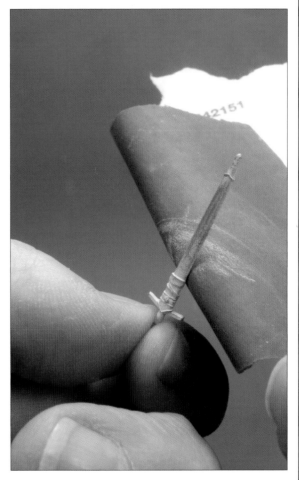

I drilled a hole about 2cm directly up into the leg, keeping the drill as straight as possible. Once it was in position, I unscrewed the drill chuck from the bit; the pin bit itself remains and acts as the permanent post. A small dab of superglue where the drill bit and heel meet guarantees that the bit will not slip out of the hole.

Very fine sandpaper (300 grit) is used to remove flash and smooth out rough surfaces. White metal is quite soft so it is best to sandpaper lightly and repeatedly rather than to attempt quick, vigorous sanding.

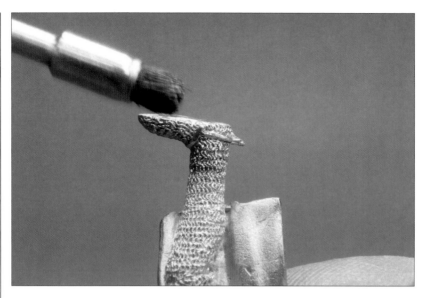

LEFT With a synthetic brush attached to my drill, I lightly polished all areas that will be metallic in the finished product. I do not paint metallic parts because metal on its own makes for the best metallic finish. The areas that received a polishing on this figure included the chain mail, helmet, leggings, and axe blade. Note the difference between the foot and ankle, which has been polished, and the unpolished chain mail on the upper leg.

RIGHT Some of the parts are glued in place using a small amount of five-minute epoxy. Sometimes, the 'five minutes' can turn into 15 minutes and one develops very cramped fingers from holding parts in one place for extended periods. One trick to speed the process up is to dab a small drop of superglue into the joint while the epoxy glue is drying. The chemical reaction instantaneously sets the epoxy.

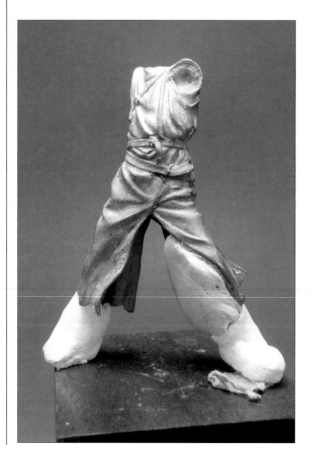

LEFT I have added automotive-repair putty to fill in the gaps and voids and applied Tamiya liquid glue to smooth out the putty while it is still wet. All areas that will be metallic in finish have been covered with a white adhesive tacky putty. I have opted to leave off the shield, head, arms, axe and sword and will paint these later on in the process, as these can more easily be painted off the figure in the finishing process.

The figure is primed in two even but light coats of Citadel White primer. Once the primer is dry, the adhesive white putty is then removed.

The primer is dry and the figure is ready for the painting process.

Scratch-building

Sculpting and scratch-building figures require new skills, and an entire book could be devoted to this particular topic. There are many books on the subject and buying one is well worth the investment. Although this subject can hardly be covered in great depth in a few pages, there are a few important notes to consider when embarking on a scratch-building project.

One of the most important rules for scratch-building figures is grasping the concept of proportions and using the length of the head as a standard unit against which to measure all other parts of the body. For instance, a whole human figure is 7½–8 head-lengths high and 2⅓ heads wide at its widest point. Once this has been determined, all other measurements can be related to it. It is widely recommended that a diagram be put on paper in scale to keep the pose and stance in context during the construction phase.

The first stage in a scratch-building project is to make an armature, or, 'skeleton' of the figure, which will give the figure strength and provide a strong basis on which to build. A thin soft wire (e.g. paperclips) is used for this purpose and will allow for adjustments to position the limbs. Following this, several layers of putty are added, covering the wire armature and building the thickness of the body. The most popular medium currently available for scratch-building figures is Milliput epoxy putty. This is a two-part material which is mixed – or kneaded – and can be moulded, sculpted, and shaped before it dries in 1 to 1½ hours. Once it dries it can be carved, filed and sanded to precise shapes. In the accompanying images, French modeller Gregory Girault shares a scratch-building project of a 54mm Highlander overleaf, to provide a visual on the steps he took to complete his project.

RIGHT The first step was building an armature. Greg built his armature using flexible wire and Fimo putty. Fimo is a brand of clay, which once baked for about 30 minutes at 110°C will harden. Other alternatives are Milliput Putty or A & B Putty. The armature was worked by bending the wires and ensuring that the torso and the movement of the figure were anatomically correct.

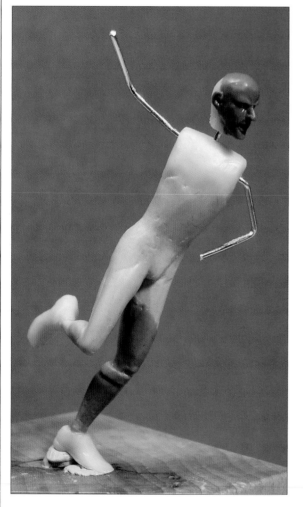

LEFT The armature was then filled with a 'bulk layer' using Milliput, using rolled out and well-kneaded thin layers one at a time, and then rubbing the epoxy with a wet finger to smooth out rough surfaces and shape the forms of the figure. Milliput is very tacky in the initial stages and constantly dampening your fingers in water (or baby oil) helps avoid this stickiness. Milliput usually fully hardens within 3–4 hours.

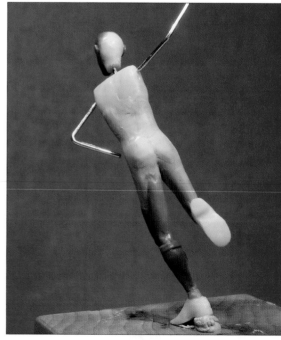

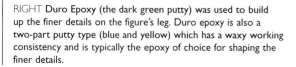

RIGHT Duro Epoxy (the dark green putty) was used to build up the finer details on the figure's leg. Duro epoxy is also a two-part putty type (blue and yellow) which has a waxy working consistency and is typically the epoxy of choice for shaping the finer details.

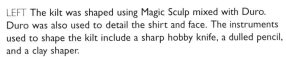

LEFT The kilt was shaped using Magic Sculp mixed with Duro. Duro was also used to detail the shirt and face. The instruments used to shape the kilt include a sharp hobby knife, a dulled pencil, and a clay shaper.

RIGHT The pleats were shaped by carefully scribing a dulled knife into the kilt to give the effect of overlapping folds.

LEFT Duro was used to shape and detail the face and to add texture to the hair. Most modellers who scratch-build a figure will use Duro to shape the face, hair, hands and small fine details on a uniform (note the buttons on the front of the figure's jacket).

The sword was detailed with Duro mixed with Magic Sculp and carefully scribed with a dulled hobby blade.

The sporran, the revolver handle, buttons and inscription on the belt plate were made using Duro. The light green parts are Magic Sculp.

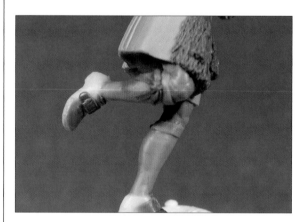

The hose ribbons and the shoe-buckles were sculpted from Duro.

Note the attention given to the pleats.

The completed 54mm figure ready for primer.

Painting and finishing

Introduction

Many enthusiasts shudder at the thought of having to paint a figure. While the construction process requires a series of engineering and mechanical skills, painting figures requires artistic and creative skills. These are two very different skill sets. Despite this difference, I am a firm believer that anyone can paint a figure well, but it takes patience, practice and, most importantly, the following of some straightforward guidelines. While patience and practice cannot be learned from this manual, easy-to-understand explanations of the most important and basic fundamentals for painting figures can be shared through visual images and carefully written explanations.

There are many types of brushes and it is beneficial to have several in your collection. One does not have to spend huge amounts of money on decent brushes. Popular mid-range brushes include Aqualflex, Nobel Gold, Premier, and Galleria.

The key to finding a good brush is sourcing one that has a nicely tapered point. Good care of brushes takes a few minutes – properly soak down your brushes and wipe off residue paint on a rag. Paintbrushes are best stored in a jar or glass in an upright position with the bristles on top.

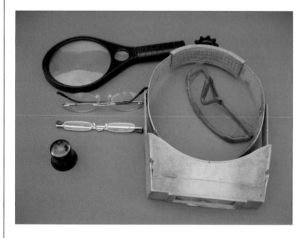

Good eyewear can include inexpensive reading glasses (+1.50 –2.00), an Optivisor, a jeweller's loop and a magnifying glass.

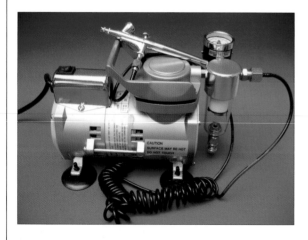

An airbrush can be very helpful in painting a basecoat on figures to provide a smooth and even surface on which to work.

Before starting on the actual painting process, there are a few important tools you will need for painting. Let us begin with paintbrushes. Much can be written about brushes. Some will argue: 'Buy the best you can afford', while others will say: 'Buy brushes for your intended purposes.' I fall into the latter group, because I tend to believe that results will depend only partly on the quality of your brush and to a larger extent on your ability to use the brush. In a similar way, a top-of-the-line airbrush is only as good as its user.

There are hundreds of brushes on the market, with prices ranging from very cheap to the obscenely expensive. Brushes are made with natural bristle, natural hair or synthetic fibres. Bristle hair and natural hair are similar in many respects, but have two major differences: natural hair has a single individual point, while bristle has a number of natural tips, which makes the bristles less flexible but more durable. The key to finding a very good brush is less about picking the brush with the smallest tuft of hairs or longest life, and more about finding a brush that has a nicely tapered point. Most of the brushes I purchase at my local art store are good quality, and for the price of one expensive sable brush, I am able to purchase five or six synthetic brushes that will probably last two to three years. If one of my 'no name' brand brushes is accidentally left on my workbench full of paint and dries out completely, my replacement cost is minimal. As an added point, oils and enamels are not typically harsh on brushes, and, with proper care, any brush should last a very long time.

An equally important piece of equipment is some form of eyewear magnification. Working with figures requires considerable concentration. The exacting nature of the hobby demands some added visual aid. To avoid straining and squinting, invest in a decent pair of reading glasses that can be purchased at most drug stores. Alternatively, there are various companies that offer eyepiece magnifiers, such as the Optivisor. This contraption has true optical glass lenses that resist scratching and can be worn over regular prescription glasses. I have found that the best standard magnification is a '5' (the 5 stands for 5 dioptre magnification). Other powers (2, 3, 4, 7, 10) are also available, but are either too weak (2, 3 and 4), to the point where one is still straining to focus, or too strong (7, 10), resulting in headaches over long painting sessions. Of course, much depends on the individual.

This chapter will cover in general terms the three primary paint types used for painting figures: oils, enamels and acrylics. The universal question often pondered is which paint type is best and most suited for painting figures. There is no hard and fast answer to this question, but here are a few points to keep in mind. The main difference between acrylics and either oil or enamel paints is the drying time. Oils and enamels allow for more time to blend colours while

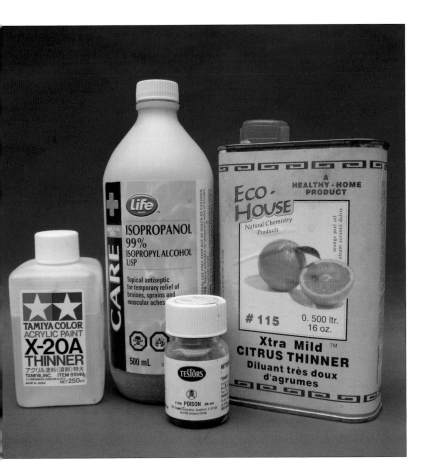

Paint thinners can also act as paint cleaners. For acrylic paint, tap water, Tamiya thinners or isopropyl alcohol work best. For enamels and oils, I use Testor's thinners or a local brand with similar properties. Acrylic paint cannot be cleaned with Testor's thinners and oil and enamel paints cannot be cleaned with water or isopropyl alcohol-based thinners.

acrylics require layering of paint to achieve a blending effect. The slow drying aspect of oils and enamels can be considered an advantage (for the beginner and intermediate modeller) where errors can be corrected, while others may regard this as an impediment for the modeller who prefers to work fast and see instant results.

Acrylic paint is generally non-removable when it is dry, although isopropyl alcohol can lift some fresh paint films. This makes it difficult to correct errors. Acrylic paints also require distinct techniques. The fast drying time forces the acrylic painter to work at a much faster pace than an oil or enamel painter. On the other hand, acrylic paints offer a wide range of colours and tones, and mixing paints is not necessarily required. Depending on the type of acrylic paint you opt to use, these can be relatively inexpensive, very accessible and the nature of acrylics makes them non-toxic.

Painting colourful uniforms will pose new challenges and the results can really pay off with some experimenting and trying new techniques.

27

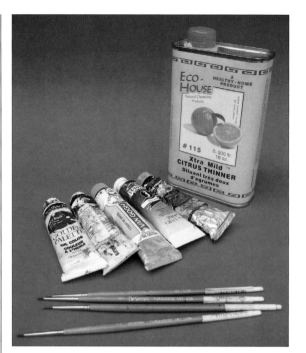

This is all it takes to get going with painting with oils – a few brushes, some tubes of paint and an enamel thinner.

Working with oil paints

Artists' oils are slow-drying paints consisting of pigment suspended in a drying oil. Popular brands include Winsor & Newton, Rembrandt, Old Holland and Van Gogh. Oil paints are hard-wearing and offer luminous colours. The slow drying time allows you to physically blend the wet colours in a subtle way. Drying time is determined primarily by the amount of carrier (linseed oil) contained in a tube. The drying time can be reduced by first placing the oil paint on a sheet of paper for about an hour to allow excess linseed oil to be absorbed before application.

One of the advantages of oil paints is the limited number of colours you need to start. Essentially, with a good basic selection, it is possible to mix any combination of paint to achieve any colour tone. My inventory includes Flake White, Ivory Black, Burnt Umber, Raw Sienna, Gold Ochre and Yellow Ochre.

Oil paints present the unique challenge of learning the principles of the colour wheel. Because the number of oil colours available is smaller than acrylics or enamels, an artist's colour wheel helps you better understand how to achieve a wide range of colours. A colour wheel is based on the three primary colours – red, yellow and blue – that cannot be mixed by any combination of other colours. All other colours are derived from these three. This is important, because a modeller will need to have some grasp of paint combinations and mixes to achieve a specific colour. This comes with practice. Visual guides such as a colour wheel can be purchased from most art stores.

Oil paints are expensive, compared with acrylics or enamels. What determines the price is the cost of mixing the paint, not the cost of the pigment. Paint manufacturers have a choice between coarsely ground or finely ground

Different brands of oil paints can be mixed together without any reaction. These are some of the better quality oil paints on the market – Winton paints by Winsor & Newton (less expensive), Rembrandt, Van Gogh, and high-quality Winsor & Newton offerings (which are obviously more expensive).

The three paints that I used exclusively for this Andrea 54mm metal knight are Van Gogh Titanium White, Lukas Studios Ivory Black and Coerulium Blue by Rowney Georgian.

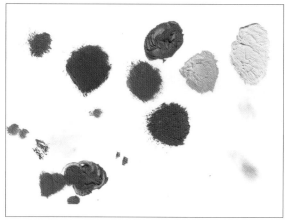

My colour palette used these three colours exclusively. Mixing the three colours in varying ratios created lighter and darker shades.

pigments. Coarsely ground pigments are much easier and less time-consuming to mill. Although oil paints are expensive, one tube should last a modeller a lifetime.

Applying oil paint is quite different from applying acrylics, but closely related to using enamels. For this reason, many enamel painters find the transition to oil paints almost painless. In fact, most enamel painters will also use oils for certain tasks. Oils and enamels require thin applications, and the blending process of one wet colour into another provides stunning results.

The difference between enamels and oils is that enamels will typically dry in 15 to 20 minutes while oil paints will begin to dry in 15 to 20 hours. Both enamel and oil paints can easily be intermixed without any adverse effects and, in fact,

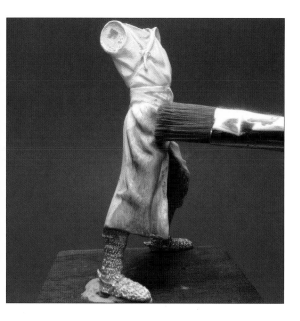

The figure has been primed in white. My base colour was a mix of Coerulium Blue by Rowney Georgian mixed with Van Gogh Titanium White in a ratio of 4:1 – that is, four parts blue to one part white.

Once the paint is applied, I remove the excess paint by lightly dragging and removing the excess paint and leaving a very thin coat of paint on the surface. The paint is so thin that you can see the white primer underneath.

I applied highlights on the tops of all folds and on any area that protrudes from the surface of the figure's uniform. My highlight mix is the base colour mixed with 20 per cent Titanium White.

I added a second highlight on top of the freshly applied first highlights; however, this time I added 20 per cent more Titanium White to my paint mix.

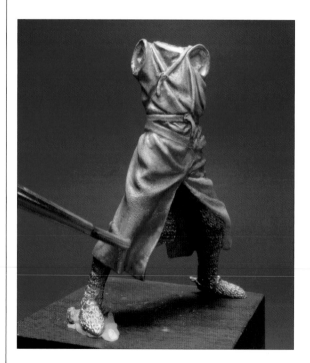

While all three applications of paint are wet – that is, base, first highlight and second highlight – I use the wet-on-wet blending technique of lightly jabbing and stippling a rounded dry-brush onto the border between each layer of paint.

As I continue to stipple my brush onto the highlight points, the paint begins to blend itself and blurs any sharp contrasts between the different colours that I have applied.

mixing both paint medium types will increase the drying time of enamels, while offering a wider spectrum of hues and tones than using oils alone.

In the following step-by-step, I will share the most basic, common techniques and approach to using oils on the garment of an Andrea Miniatures 54mm knight. This approach calls for using three important techniques: basecoat, highlights and shadows, and blending.

After priming a figure (preferably with a white primer), you have the option of immediately applying oils, or applying an acrylic or enamel basecoat of a lighter, complementary colour to the finished tone. Some modellers opt to airbrush the basecoat to guarantee a consistent, smooth surface. However, for this project, I chose to use oil paints exclusively for my basecoat.

The first step is to place a blob of oil paint the size of a large pea on a sheet of typing paper. Allow the paper to absorb the excess linseed oil. After about an hour, the oil paint is slightly pasty. With a 1cm-wide brush, I applied an overall coat of a mix of Coerulium Blue mixed with Van Gogh Titanium White in a ratio of 4:1. The paint is applied always ensuring that all of the nooks and crannies receive a thin application of paint. I do not add retarders or thinners. The application should be thin enough to allow you to literally see the primer through the paint. I used a soft dry brush to remove the excess paint by flicking the brush in a light downward motion.

Once the first basecoat had dried completely (2–3 days), I repeated the same process using the precise same amount of oil paint: I applied a light coat and used the flicking technique to remove excess paint. You will notice that the base became slightly darker in tone, and any area where the primer was visible has been covered. While the second thin layer of paint was still wet, I began the process of adding highlights, using the 'wet-on-wet' technique to blend the colours. I usually start with highlights because it is easier to cover mistakes by adding a darker colour over a lighter colour.

To add highlights, I applied 20 per cent Titanium White oil paint to the base colour on my palette and then painted in thin lines using a fine tapered #0 brush on all of the highlight points protruding from the surface. The most frequent locations for adding highlights are the tops of creases, the tops of shoulders, and the knees and along folds. Directing a table lamp down from above a figure helps identify areas that should have highlights.

Once the highlights have been applied, I start the meticulous and time-consuming process of blending the highlight paint into the wet base paint. Blending requires lightly stippling and jabbing a dry, small, rounded brush onto the border points between the freshly applied highlight paint and the underlying semi-dry wet base. The purpose of this step is to alter the stark border between the lighter highlight colour and the darker base colour, to a middle ground colour which combines (in this case) both the darker base blue and lighter highlight blue. On this figure, it took me about 20 minutes to blend the highlights. I repeated the very same step for the second highlights by adding 20 per cent more white to my highlight mix.

For the shadowing process, I mixed up a darker paint by adding 15 per cent Ivory Black to the base colour. This darker paint was applied to all the shadow areas with a '1' brush. I allowed the figure to sit for about two hours (under an overturned glass to protect it from dust). I then started the blending process using a clean, dry, #2 brush. I lightly stroked the brush on the border between the semi-wet base colour and the freshly applied shadow paint. Because all of the work was being done while the oils were wet, there was no need to use thinners to help blend the two colours. This process took about 45 minutes. I repeated the same step, this time adding another 10 per cent Ivory Black to my shadow paint mix, applying it within the borders of the previous shadow paint and blending it in. The figure was left to dry for about one week.

On this particular figure, I applied two highlights and three shadows. However, one could add more highlights and shadows – each one lighter or

I repeat the same steps for the shading by adding 15 per cent Ivory Black to the base colour and stippling this inside all of the shaded areas.

I repeated the very same step but this time, I added another 10 per cent Ivory Black to my paint mix and painted in the very deepest areas within the borders of the first shaded application. The blending process is repeated by jabbing and stippling the border between the first shadow and second darker shadow.

With a large rounded brush, I lightly whisk the surface of the figure in a downward motion to remove any excess paint and further blend the wet paints in the surface.

I decided to add another shadow in selective locations with 10 per cent more Ivory Black in the shadow colour mix and added this into the deepest recesses. With a rounded dry brush, I lightly whisked the surface again of the figure to blend the colours to ensure that there are no stark borders between highlights and shadows.

A light jabbing motion with the brush removes any small blemishes. The oil paint was left to dry for a week before applying Testor's Dullcote. Once completely dry, the rest of the painting process could continue.

darker than earlier coats – to provide more depth. When the oils are perfectly dry, you may notice a slight satin sheen or eggshell finish. This is a normal property of oil paints. A few light oversprays of a flat clear coat such as Tamiya Flat Clear or Testor's Dullcote will reduce the sheen. It is critical to ensure the oils are perfectly dry first, otherwise the matt coat combined with even the slightest wet oil paint will result in a permanently glossy finish on your figure. For this reason, painting in oils requires time and patience.

Don't be discouraged if all of the meticulous work you put into highlighting and shadowing is not evident during the painting session. This is because the natural glossy effect of wet oil paint tends to obliterate the contrast between highlights and shadows. However, when the oil paint dries completely – and even more so when you apply a few squirts of a flat clear – the contrast between highlights and shadows will become very evident.

The completed figure.

Painting a shield

The figure's shield was first polished up using fine sandpaper to remove any grime and dust particles on the surface.

The shield was primed with Tamiya primer in two light coats.

After applying a white Vallejo acrylic paint for the base with a brush, I cut thin strips of Tamiya tape to cover the area that I wanted to protect from subsequent paint.

I sprayed two light coats of Tamiya Red from an aerosol canister. The second coat of red should only be applied after the first application of red has thoroughly dried. Ensure not to make the application too heavy, otherwise a paint build-up will occur along the ridge of the tape.

The tape was carefully removed after the paint had completely dried.

A wash of Winsor & Newton Raw Umber oil paint was applied to the shield to tone down the colours and provide a weathered effect.

I applied a very thin amount of black oil paint on paper and pressed the blade of an X-acto knife into the paint, and then carefully placed the blade onto the shield to denote slashes and cuts.

A few applications of dry pigments were applied to depict a semi battle-worn shield.

35

The primary Humbrol paints I will use to paint the red tunic. The ratio mix of my base paint will be 3:1 of Humbrol Matt Scarlet #60 and Matt Red Brown #100. I will also use Matt Wine #73 as my shadows medium and # 61 Flesh as my highlighting medium.

Working with enamel paints

The most popular enamel brand for painting figures is Humbrol. This range offers a wide variety of colours in gloss, clear, matt, satin, metallic and metalcote varieties. Humbrol paints come in 14ml tins designed for easy application. Other enamel brands include Testors and ModelMaster.

Enamel paints are generally inexpensive, and readily available at most hobby stores. The large range of khakis, greys and drab colours, particularly in the Humbrol line, make these particularly useful for painting modern figures. Enamel paints dry rock hard and typically offer one-coat coverage.

Similar to oils, enamels requires the modeller to physically blend a colour into surrounding wet paint, achieving a subtle gradation. However, the time frame to do this is only about 15 to 20 minutes. Fortunately, oil and enamel paints can easily be mixed together to broaden the colour range and help lengthen the drying time. The slower drying of oils and enamels can be considered an advantage (for the beginner and intermediate modeller) to allow errors to be corrected. However, the modeller who prefers to work fast and see instant results may regard this as an impediment.

With enamels, the approach is very similar to oils, but several techniques can be added. On this 54mm Elite Miniatures figure – a Black Watch 42nd Highlander Crimean War soldier – I will apply two shadows and one highlight to the tunic. It is also possible to apply five or six different shades of each by adding smaller amounts of lighter paint per application for the highlights, and smaller amounts of a darker paint for each application of the shadows. It is really up to you to decide what you feel is adequate to attain good results.

The process may seem long and tedious for such subtle effects, but this is the ideal situation – particularly for painting with reds, yellows and whites. Understated effects are far more attractive and appealing than overdone effects. The most important tip is to take your time when applying the highlights and shadows, and keep the stippling and poking

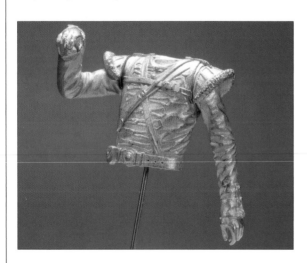

A few select brushes ('00', '0' and '1'), a few tins of selected Humbrol enamel paints and some Testor's thinners is all that I require to paint this figure.

The figure's arms have been glued to the torso using 5-minute epoxy.

The torso of the figure was primed with two light coats of Tamiya White primer. I drilled a small hole in the underside to accommodate a temporary post for handling the part.

motion light and consistent when blending the borders of each application. The stippling motion can be time-consuming and test your patience, but it is the one step that will make all of the difference to your figure's overall appearance.

To start on the red tunic, I placed on my palette (a simple plastic sheet) small amounts of Humbrol enamel Matt Scarlet #60 and Matt Red Brown #100. I mixed these two colours in a 3:1 ratio to provide a dark red base colour. When using Humbrols, it is best not to shake the tin to mix the paint. The murky mass that accumulates at the bottom of the tin is ideal for brush painting. I transferred a small amount of this chunky mass with a toothpick from each tin to my palette. I mixed the two colours, and applied the mix to the tunic using a #1 flat brush, always moving the brush in a vertical, downward motion.

Once the first base layer was dry (20 minutes or so), I reapplied a second thin coat to the tunic using the same colour mix, consistency and amount as the first application. This second coat of base paint ensures that all of the white primed areas have been fully covered, and eliminates brush strokes from the first application. As soon as the second coat of paint was applied, I immediately moved to the shading and highlighting process of the tunic.

The shading and highlighting of a figure is truly the critical step to bring the figure to life. Applying shades and highlights compensates for the lack of adequate light on a scale figure. This is particularly evident in a badly lit model showroom, where the lighting will either be too faint to allow a viewer to distinguish details on a figure, or too strong, which washes out any subtle highlights and shadows. Some modellers prefer to apply shadows using a series of washes – similar to washes applied on armour models. While this may work sometimes, there are several other effective and risk-free approaches to creating shadows and highlights.

The technique I have used in this feature for the jacket begins with two different shadow types – medium shadows and deep shadows. On my palette, I added 10 per cent Humbrol Matt Wine #73 to my base colour and mixed this up with a large brush. With a well-tapered #0 brush, I applied a thin layer of the medium shadow paint into and inside all the folds and recesses of the tunic. If you have trouble identifying the shadow areas, shine a lamp or flashlight directly down from above the figure to determine where the shadows fall. The medium shadow paint should be placed in any area that looks like a small dip or depression on the surface. On a typical figure, about 50 per cent of the area being painted will generally take the medium shadow shade.

As soon as the first medium shadow was applied, the next step is the blending of the medium shade into the semi-wet base. At this point, the second base coat is almost dry, but still workable. Blending the medium

A first application of the enamel paint mix (3:1 ratio Matt Scarlet #60 and Matt Red Brown #100) has been applied to the tunic and was left to dry for two hours.

A second basecoat of the same mix was applied to remove the streak brush marks from the first application, to provide an even finish to the tunic and help eliminate any areas where the white primer was still evident.

As soon as the second base was applied, I began the process of painting in the first shadow colours. The first shadow colour is a mix of the base colour with 10 per cent Matt Wine 73 added in my base colour mix.

A thinner-moist 'I' brush was then lightly stippled on the border between the freshly applied shadow paint with the adjacent base colour. The stippling process is a series of small jabs using the end of the brush's hairs to loosen and mix the paints. The result of the stippling action is a third colour combining the shadow tone and the base tone to create a blurred combination of the two tones. This process is called blending.

A second application of a darker shadow tone was added by mixing in 50 per cent more Matt Wine to the paint mix and added inside the border of the first shadow application. It may only require a thin line to be painted directly inside the very tight folds of the arms to denote the second shadow. I used a '00' brush for this application.

shadows into the base requires using a clean, #1 brush moistened with thinner to lightly poke and jab the border between the semi-dry base colour and the freshly applied wet medium shadow. The small amount of thinner in the brush will loosen up the base paint just enough to blend the freshly applied medium shadow, creating a 'middle' shade that results in a tone that combines the basecoat and the medium shadow. This process of stippling the brush onto the shadow borders was executed all the way around the tunic.

Once the first medium shadows were applied and blended, I moved to the application of the deeper shadows. For the deeper shadows, I added 50 per cent more Humbrol enamel #73 to my original base colour, and added the deep shadow paint with a small, pointed #00 brush to the deepest section of the medium shadows, always within the borders of the freshly applied medium shadows. In very narrow folds, it may only be necessary to paint a thin line to represent the deep shadow areas. Once the deep shadows were applied,

A thinner-moist brush was again used to blend the outer borders of the first shadow and the second shadow using a light jabbing motion. Once this was applied, I allowed the paint to dry thoroughly overnight.

The next step was adding some highlights to accentuate the outer folds on the figure's tunic. For this process, I mixed up another batch of the base colour and added 15 per cent Humbrol 'Flesh'. I rarely use white as a highlighting agent because it is too harsh. Instead, I try to find a colour that is complementary to the base colour.

With a clean thinner-moist '00' brush, I carefully jabbed the highlight application to spread the paint out over a dry base coat. I also added another very thin line of shadow paint into the deepest recesses to further accentuate the contrast between shadow and highlights.

Here is the result, but under normal room lighting. As you can see, the strong contrast between the paints is no longer noticeable. This is because under regular room lighting, a figure is not subjected to intensive 200 watts of lighting. For this reason, never judge your figure from a macro image on your computer but always from regular viewing distance of about 1–2ft away from the figure.

I switched to a clean, thinner-moistened #1 round brush, and began the task of poking and lightly jabbing the border between the deep shadow and medium shadow.

After the shadows were applied and were completely dry, I started in with one application of highlights to the figure's uniform. Some modellers prefer the dry-brush method to apply highlights, and, although this can work, it is far more effective to actually paint and blend highlight colours. Dry-brushing is a technique of stroking and rubbing a minimal amount of a lighter-coloured paint onto highlight points. Unfortunately, dry-brushing can leave nasty brush marks, and the action of repeatedly rubbing a brush in a single area can result in the brush hairs polishing the base paint (particularly if the figure is white metal), which will inevitably leave a glossy or satin finish. This cannot be easily remedied with a clear flat overspray.

The technique I use for applying highlights is similar to the shadowing process, with the exception that the colour mixes being applied become lighter in tone, into the upper folds, and are applied on a dry surface otherwise known as 'wet-on-dry'. To make the highlight paint, I added about 15 per cent Matt Flesh #61 to my original base of Matt Scarlet and Matt Red Brown. With a #00 brush, I applied a thin layer of the highlight paint on all of the fold tops of the uniform. The highlight paint mix should be placed very sparingly on the top of any area that protrudes from the figure's clothing. On a typical figure, about 30 per cent of the area being painted will generally take the highlight paint application. As soon as the highlight paint was applied, I began the process of blending the paint. However, the base colour had now fully cured, and instead of physically blending the highlight paint, I opted to poke and jab a brush moistened with thinners on the highlight borders to diffuse and spread the edges of the fresh highlight paint. By carefully jabbing my brush on the highlight paint borders, the paint was spread out leaving a feathered subtle highlight. This is called using the wet-on-dry technique. I noted that too much jabbing and blending had slowly washed out the contrast between shadow and highlight. This was the perfect opportunity to add another very thin application of a second highlight to complete the process of highlighting the colour of the scarlet jacket.

The completed figure.

Painting tartans

There are many approaches for painting the intricate and seemingly complicated tartan pattern of a kilt. It is true that the combinations of single and double tramlines crossing can confuse the eye and, hence, the patterns appear very complex.

However, the most important aspect to remember when painting a kilt is that a tartan is usually made up of nothing more than a series of intersecting lines, and the colours (aside from a few oddities) are generally very muted and dark. For instance, the Black Watch is quite a simple tartan to paint because there are only two colours – dark blue and dark green – and the tartan is so dark that one can hardly distinguish between the two colours. Here I will share with you a very simple approach for painting a Black Watch tartan.

After priming in black, I applied two light coats of Testor's Olive Green enamel from an aerosol canister.

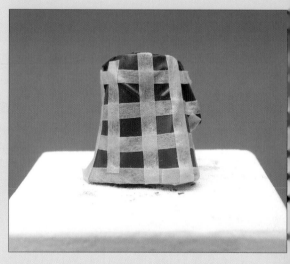

I then applied trimmed-down Tamiya tape in vertical and horizontal positions ensuring the spacing is congruent all of the way around. This acts as my template in keeping the lines as straight as possible. Make use of reference photos to determine where lines cross.

I airbrushed Tamiya German Dark Grey acrylics in two very light coats all of the way around the kilt.

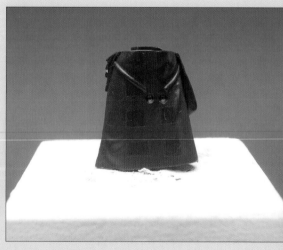

Once the paint was fully cured, I removed the tape to reveal a grid that would serve as my template.

All boxed areas were then painted in with a lighter tone of the green shade using a tapered brush.

I then applied three heavy washes of Winsor & Newton Lamp Black oil paint mixed with thinners. Once the washes had thoroughly dried, I drew in lines separating the boxes with Matt Black enamel paint.

All of the primary lines have been added, and two more washes of Lamp Black oil paint were added to the tartan. One should apply several dark washes until the tonal value between the green and blue is barely noticeable. The Black Watch kilts are very dark and this should be replicated in scale format as well.

In applying another black wash, I inadvertently washed away most of the black lines. I should have waited another hour or so until the enamel paint had thoroughly dried. The tone is correct, but some of the lines are missing.

I decided to use another approach for applying the lines – this time with a architect's .01 black felt pen. Although the lines will waver up and down and may not be very straight, this will not be noticeable at regular viewing distance. Once the felt pen ink has dried, I applied two coats of Testor's Dullcote to complete the project.

Working with acrylic paints

There are many brands of acrylic paints for painting figures. The more common paints for brush-painting used by figure modellers are Vallejo, Citadel, Jo Sonya, Golden Artist Colours and Liquitex. These acrylic paints are water-soluble, fast drying, provide good coverage and offer a wide range of colours. Some brands, such as Vallejo, have the added characteristic of not leaving brush marks, which is a common trait with some other acrylics, such as Gunze or Tamiya (both of these are meant for airbrushing and not recommended for intricate brushwork).

The downside to acrylics is that they will wear down your brushes more quickly than oils or enamels. Cleaning your brushes thoroughly with an appropriate brush cleaner (such as Tamiya acrylic thinner) is a must after using acrylic paint. Acrylics need to be well mixed before use. Most problems occur in the opening painting stages because the paint is not well mixed. To remedy this, always mix the paint before and during your painting session to ensure that all of the pigment at the bottom of the bottle is mixed into the liquid carrier.

Another important aspect of painting with acrylics is the proper thinning ratio of paint to water. These are not paints that should be used directly out of the bottle. For basecoating a figure, the ratio of acrylic paint to water should be approximately 1:1 – that is, one drop of paint for every drop of water. For

All of the necessary materials to paint a figure in acrylics. The large plastic tray is used to mix my paints and the metal trays are used for the thinning agent (water). I also make use of eyedroppers to ensure that the paint to water ratio is accurate. The proper thinning ratio of paint to water is critical.

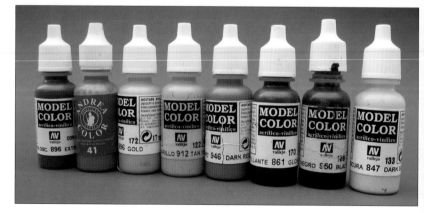

Vallejo paints are probably the most popular acrylic paints on the market for figure painting, and the best acrylic medium for military figures given the large number of paints in the series.

For my subject, I chose a superbly cast resin 120mm Miniature Alliance Vietcong figure. Most of the parts were glued in place with 5-minute epoxy.

I primed the figure in Tamiya White primer and set it aside to dry thoroughly (30 minutes). This allowed me to better see the surface and clean up any blemishes and seams that I had not noticed in the construction process.

outlining and painting small details, the ratio changes to one drop of paint for two drops of water. For highlighting and shading, the ratio changes to a more transparent coat, attained by mixing one drop of paint to three or four drops of water. Most modellers use an eyedropper to help mix the paint more accurately to the consistency required.

The one characteristic that sets acrylic paints apart from enamels and oils is their quick drying time. This does not allow for the physical blending of paints. With enamels and oils, the border between two colours is blended by mixing them while wet on the surface to achieve a 'middle ground' colour. With acrylics, the process calls for adding layers of transparent coats – one on top of the other – to give the visual effect of blending. Adding several successive applications of thinned acrylic paint over a specific area will result in the gradual build up of various tones. As any aircraft or armour modeller will know, an overall wash of a darker thinned enamel or oil paint over a surface will render the overall tonal value of the surface slightly darker. The process with acrylics is very similar, with the exception that the thinning agent is water and the application – termed 'layering' for this purpose – is placed specifically on highlight and shadow areas only.

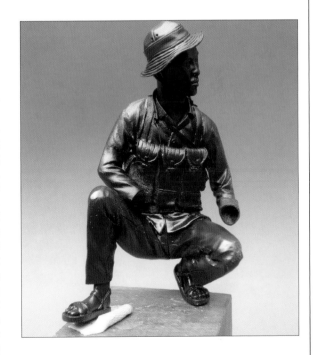

The figure was then primed in one light coat of Citadel Black primer. This is an excellent primer that will allow you to begin working from a surface that is perfectly uniform in colour.

The three colours I will mix to achieve a base colour for the shirt – Vallejo Dark Seagreen, Extra Dark Green and Russian Uniform Green. Once mixed in a 2:1:1 ratio, I added 50 per cent water for my base mix.

I should point out that I am not a proficient acrylic painter. However, as a newcomer to this new-found paint, I have discovered some important tricks that I will share with you in my step-by-step.

For my subject, I chose a 120mm Miniature Alliance Vietcong figure. To start off the painting process, I primed the figure and allowed this to dry thoroughly. For the shirt, I mixed Vallejo Dark Green, Extra Dark Green and Russian Uniform Green in a 2:1:1 ratio and this was further mixed with the same amount of water. I applied two coats of the base to the shirt with a wide 1cm paintbrush and allowed this to dry. Once the base paint had completely dried (about five minutes) on the shirt, I turned to the highlighting and shading process.

I started with the shading stage of the shirt, and for this exercise I used the layering technique where I applied several progressively thinner coats of a darker diluted paint one on top of the other. The transparency of the shadow paint is critical and the build-up of several transparent shadows results in a darker tone. I mixed my first shade using the same base colour I used for the shirt and added 10 per cent Vallejo Matt Black in the mix and diluted the paint mix with three times more water. The mix should look like tinted water. I applied the diluted paint with a tapered brush into all areas where the least amount of light will reach. By touching my brush into the shadow area, the paint will capillary – or run – into the shallow areas on the surface. The amount of paint on your brush should be minimal, but enough to allow some paint to run off the bristles and onto the figure. It is worth having a 'tester' figure on hand to determine the consistency and wetness of your brush before applying the paint to your in-progress figure.

I added a second shadow by placing a touch more black in the diluted paint and reapplying the paint to the precise same shadow areas and more precisely within the borders of the previous shadow area. The transparent nature of the paint will build up and provide a slightly darker tone than the previous coat. Adding smaller controlled 'rings' of a darker shaded colour within smaller and smaller borders will give the illusion of blended colours. I repeated this step four times in total, each time adding 10 per cent more black to my base colour.

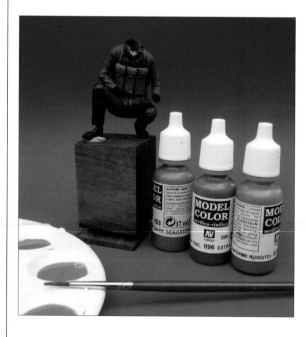

The layout as I progress through the painting process. Note that the figure has been temporarily affixed to a wooden base with Blu-Tack.

In my readings, many acrylic masters use the dry-brush method to apply acrylic highlights. I am not a huge fan of dry-brushing highlights on figures, but I cannot argue with their results and it was time to try something new. To begin the highlighting process, I mixed another batch of the shirt base colour and added 20 per cent Vallejo White to lighten up the tone. I thinned the paint by adding 30 per cent water and loaded my #1 brush with the highlight paint. I removed the excess paint on a rag and then carefully began flickering my brush on the highlight points in a back and forth motion. I repeated the same step a second time around and continued to whisk and flicker my brush by only lightly touching the highlight surfaces. I added 10 per cent Vallejo White to the first highlight paint mix and repeated the same step going around the figure twice. The highlights do not become evident and I learnt that the secret is to put the minimal amount of paint on the brush and dry-brushing repeatedly – rather than attempting to apply a heavier application of paint fewer times. I applied four dry-brush applications – each time with a little more white paint added in the base – and it was only by the last dry-brushing application that I started to notice the highlights making their appearance. This process should not be rushed and care must be taken

I applied the paint mix to the shirt with a 1cm-wide paintbrush and allowed this to dry. I applied two coats to ensure the primer was covered.

Once the base paint had completely dried (about five minutes), I started the shading stage of the shirt, and used the layering technique. This calls for applying several progressively thinner coats of a darker diluted paint one on top of the other. I mixed my first shade using the same base colour I used for the shirt and added 10 per cent Vallejo Matt Black in the mix, and diluted the paint mix with 3 times more water.

I added a second shadow by placing a touch more black in the diluted paint and reapplying the paint to the precise same shadow areas as the first application but within the borders of the previous shadow area. The transparent nature of the paint will build up and provide a slightly darker tone than the previous application.

By simply touching the brush into the shadow area, the paint will capillary into the shallow areas on the surface. Adding smaller controlled 'rings' of a darker shaded colour within smaller and smaller borders will give the illusion of blended colours.

The result after four shadow applications. I also painted the pouch on the figure's chest in Vallejo British Uniform Brown.

The shadows have been applied, and I now turned my attention to the highlights. I used the dry-brush method to apply the highlights by adding 20 per cent Vallejo White to my base shirt colour, and I thinned the paint down by adding 30 per cent water. I loaded my #1 brush with the highlight paint and whisked my brush on all of the highlight points.

I repeated the same step for the second highlight application with 10 per cent Vallejo White added to the mix, and flicked my brush on the highlight points in a light back and forth motion.

I repeated the same step two more times, each time adding another 10 per cent Vallejo White to the base colour. The highlights do not become evident, and this is favourable. The secret is to put the minimal amount of paint on the brush and lightly dry-brushing repeatedly, rather than attempting to apply a heavier application of paint in fewer goes.

o ensure the amount of the paint on the brush is kept to a bare minimum and removing any excess paint with a rag. Too much paint will ruin the effect.

If you feel that the contrast between shadows and highlights are too wide and stark, you can tone it down by applying a heavily diluted mix (10 per cent paint to 90 per cent water) of the shirt base colour to the entire clothing area to help soften the contrast and provide more balance. It should really be tinted paint and applied as evenly as possible.

As a last step on the figure's clothing, I outlined all of the details on the shirt with a mix of the base colour with black and water in 1:1:4 ratio. This mix was applied to all outlined areas with a '0' brush to help enhance and more clearly define details such as seams, pockets, lines and creases. The remainder of the figure's clothing and accessories were painted precisely in the same manner using different Vallejo paints and using the same technique as the shirt. The flesh tones were painted using oils and were applied with the wet-on-wet technique.

Using acrylics is a different medium altogether and in the hands of an experienced painter provides absolutely stunning effects and results. For more information on painting with acrylics, I do recommend Jaume Ortez and Daniel Alfonsea's book *Modelling Fallschirmjäger Figures* and Calvin Tan's *Modelling Waffen-SS Figures* – all are masters in this particular field and their books provide superbly well-written details on their respective approaches.

The results after the shading and highlighting process. The slight appearance of a sheen will be eliminated once the paint has thoroughly dried and the figure receives a light spray of Dullcote.

The completed figure. The remainder of the figure's clothing and accessories were painted precisely in the same manner using different Vallejo paints. I also added pastels to dirty the shirt and trousers. The flesh tones were painted using oils and were applied using the wet-on-wet technique.

Painting horses

Painting horses will be one of the most gratifying of all scale figure projects. As difficult to paint as horses may appear, they are not hard to do if you have the correct techniques under your belt. Some prefer to use an airbrush while others blend in a series of highlights and shadows. I have tried all of the techniques and I will share with you one technique that I found quite easy with very good results.

For this project, I will apply the 'glazing' technique using artists' oil paints. This is the process of applying very thin successive layers of a transparent paint over a dry surface and allowing the paint underneath to be visible. By repeatedly applying thin layers of oil paints on top of a dry surface and removing excess paint, the highlights remain light in tone while surrounding areas become darker. Similarly, adding paint into shaded areas will result in the deepest crevices retaining a darker tone while the area around the deepest points take on a lighter tone. This process eliminates the time-consuming task of physically blending the borders between highlights and shades on a relatively large surface area. This may be considered the 'lazy' approach, but I have had quite good results with this process and would like to share this with you. As a side note, this technique can also be used to paint leathers, belts, rifle butts, wood and footwear. Of course, you will want to further develop this particular technique to suit your own tastes and effects.

I took several photographs of a horse near my home. Having good image references on hand is very helpful for painting a subject that one does not see every day.

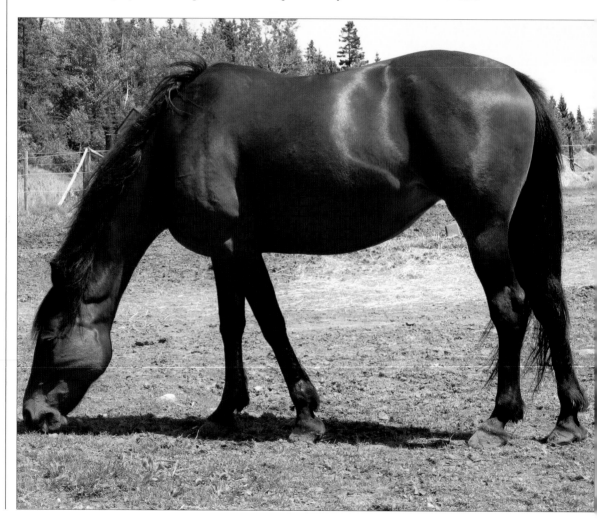

I used a 1/35th-scale horse from the Italeri Cossack set #352. The horse has been glued with Tamiya liquid glue, and putty has been used to fill in small gaps between joints.

A Tamiya White primer was applied to allow subsequent paint to adhere to the surface.

A light spray of Tamiya Matt White mixed with Tamiya thinners in a 50:50 ratio was applied to the entire horse. Note how the rump is very white while the underside is slightly darker in shade.

49

I applied a copious amount of Winsor & Newton Burnt Sienna oil paint to the whole horse. While the paint was still wet, I whisked off the excess paint with a wide brush, drawing the brush in a downward motion to follow the normal growth of hair on a horse. Note that the paint is so thinly applied that one can still see the white base underneath. The paint is left to dry under an upturned glass for about three days.

I repeated the very same step as previously using the same colour and technique. The result is a slightly darker shade of Burnt Sienna oil paint. Note how the highlight points remain quite light in tone while the shadows have begun to take on a slightly darker hue. The shadow areas become darker because the whisking motion deposits excess paint into all recesses. I allowed this to dry for five days.

The same technique was used with a third application of Burnt Sienna. The paint is quite glossy when it is wet, but will dull down as it dries.

I proceeded with the same technique, but this time I switched paints to a complementary but darker tone using a mix of Burnt Sienna and Raw Umber in a 1:2 ratio.

I repeated the same step as the preceding one, by smearing Raw Umber oils neat all over the horse and removing the excess with a wide brush. However, to capture the colour tone of my subject, the horse's coat will need to be slightly darker.

I applied yet another mix of Raw Umber into the deepest crevices and shadows of the horse. Once these were applied, I whisked a wide brush over the area to spread out excess paint. I also painted the mane, tail and socks using Humbrol Matt Black.

The horse's coat was complete and I now turned to details. The horse's mane and tail were painted again in Humbrol Matt Black and the leg stockings were airbrushed in Tamiya NATO Black. All leather straps were lightly painted with Humbrol Matt Ochre 83. The hooves were painted in Humbrol Medium Grey. I also painted the eyes and saddle with black oil paint. All that is left to do is to find a rider.

Modelling a mounted knight

At this stage, I want to bring together most of the techniques that have been covered so far in this manual and demonstrate how these various techniques can be combined to achieve a very different subject altogether. I will proceed with the assembly and painting process using step-by-step images with descriptive captions to show how I approached this project. As you will see the process is very simple and even the most novice modellers will find the approach quite straightforward and easy to accomplish. One only needs time patience and a planned approach to the steps to be taken.

The white-metal horse was cleaned up and most of the parts were glued together using 5-minute epoxy glue.

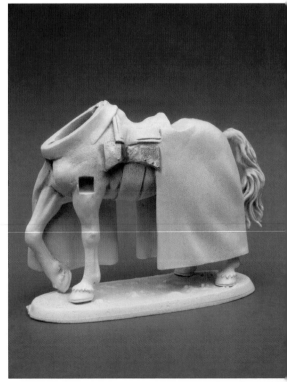

The horse was primed using Tamiya White primer with the exception of parts that would be metal in the finished product.

The horse's legs were painted using Burnt Sienna oil paints followed by Raw Umber.

LEFT Blu-Tack was applied on all metal parts that I did not want to cover in paint. The Blu-Tack should be applied after the oil paint has thoroughly dried.

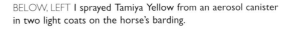

BELOW, LEFT I sprayed Tamiya Yellow from an aerosol canister in two light coats on the horse's barding.

BELOW, RIGHT I wanted to create a yellow and blue pattern on the barding, so I cut Tamiya masking tape to size and affixed this to the horse.

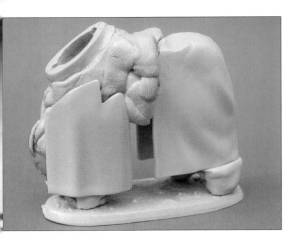

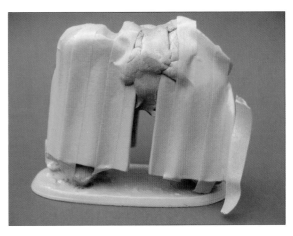

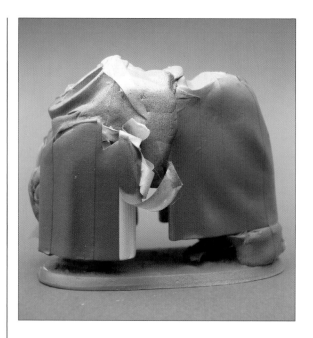

I airbrushed Tamiya XF-8 Flat Blue in two successive coats, allowing the first application to dry before executing the second application. When painting a two-colour pattern such as this, it is best to put down the lighter colour first, because applying lighter colours on top of a darker colour usually requires many applications.

The moment of truth – I removed all of the tape and Blu-Tack to reveal the basecoat.

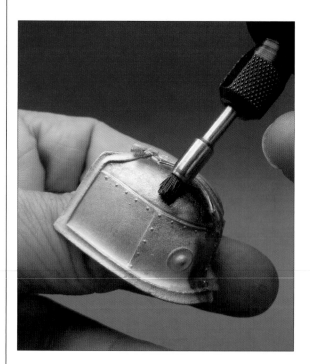

Metal armour parts were first polished up with a synthetic brush attached to a slow-speed Dremel tool. This helps clean up all residue on the surface of the metal parts and makes the metal look slightly brighter.

With an emery board, I carefully removed all blemishes and glitches around the edges of the metal parts.

To tone down the metallic parts from a mirror-polished metal to a dulled tarnished finish, I applied Lamp Black oil all over the metal parts.

I then wiped away all of the excess oil paint with a cotton swab leaving a residue of the oil paint in the crevices along the rim of the parts and around the rivets.

Note how the metal now looks very muted and worn. I allowed this to dry for two days.

Once the oil paint on the metal armour was completely dry, I airbrushed three coats of Tamiya Smoke mixed with Tamiya thinners in a 50:50 mix onto the metal parts to provide a darker finish. The metal parts were then dry-fitted to the horse.

LEFT Printer's Ink (Antique Gold by Winsor & Newton) was applied on the contour of the horse's armour and on the head armour plate to provide richness and contrast to the overall appeal of the presentation.

ABOVE For the knight, I followed the very same steps as the horse's metal armour – that is, polishing the metal, applying Lamp Black oil paint, removing the paint with a cotton swab – and airbrushed with two coats of Tamiya Smoke.

ABOVE Small details were painted using enamel paints and I airbrushed a thin mix of Tamiya Deck Tan to the horse's yellow and blue barding to help tone down the brightness of the colours. The last touch was adding some subtle earth pigments to the lower barding to further accentuate wear and weathering.

The completed model, set against a Photoshop background.

Small-scale figures

While 54mm and 1/35th-scale figures have remained at the forefront as the more popular of the scales in the modelling realm, there are several other scales that have become increasingly popular in recent times. In the smaller scales, figures can range from 2mm to 30mm, and are commonly used for miniature wargaming purposes. For many years, gamers were indifferent to the quality of the paint job. However, the 25mm, 28m and 30mm scales have increasingly become an art form of their own with improved casting techniques allowing for better paintwork.

Painting a 30mm fantasy figure

Jen Haley is an award-winning fantasy figure painter from Chicago, and here she shares her methodologies on a 30mm goblin ninja from the game 'Confrontation', produced by Rackham.

After mould lines were removed with a needle file, the figure was airbrushed with Tamiya Fine Surface primer. Jen then mixed a wash from equal parts RMS (Reaper Master Series) Brown Liner, RMS Brush-on Sealer, and water, and applied a coat directly over the white primer.

The flesh areas were base-coated with three parts Vallejo German Fieldgrey to one part RMS Brown Liner, leaving the dark wash exposed in the areas of deepest shadow.

The flesh was highlighted with Vallejo German Fieldgrey.

Jen applied a second flesh highlight of RMS Ghoul Skin, then glazed selected areas (eye sockets, tips of fingers, toes, and ears) with RMS Bruise Purple. She prefers to mix glazes with equal parts of paint and RMS Brush-on Sealer or Vallejo Matte Varnish, thinned with a small amount of water.

Jen highlighted the green flesh with RMS Moldy Skin and the purple areas with two parts RMS Rosy Skin to one part RMS Bruise Purple. The clothing was base-coated with RMS Walnut Brown.

The fleshy areas received a final highlight of equal parts RMS Blushing Rose and RMS Fair Skin. The garment and eye sockets were shaded with a glaze of pure black, and pure white was dotted into the eyes. Jen highlighted the tunic with RMS Woodstain Brown.

Next, she used three parts RMS Driftwood Brown to one part Woodstain Brown to further highlight the clothing and to basecoat the sandals, chopsticks and chest strap. Trim areas were based with RMS Chestnut Brown, and the obi with Vallejo Blue Violet.

More shadows were applied with glazes: Vallejo Burnt Umber on the wood and leather, Vallejo Violet Red on the obi. Chestnut Brown details were highlighted with RMS Rust Brown.

Another layer of highlights was applied: RMS Pale Indigo on the obi, RMS Phoenix Red on the red trim, and Driftwood on the sandals and chopsticks. Jen basecoated metal details such as the foot spikes with RMS Shadowed Stone.

Jen painted the claws with a thin layer of RMS Shadowed Stone over the initial Walnut Brown wash, and highlighted the claw tips and foot spikes with RMS Khaki Highlight. The wood and leather received a final highlight of RMS Stained Ivory, the red trim of Vallejo Sunny Skintone, and the obi a mix of equal parts RMS Pale Indigo and pure white. She then gave the base a coat of RMS Stone Grey at this point.

The flagstones on the base were glazed with Brown Liner. The poison in the vials was painted with RMS Clouded Sea and the empty space with Pale Indigo, touching the corks with RMS Driftwood Brown and the rims with RMS Stone Grey.

The Clouded Sea was shaded with RMS Stormy Sea toward the surface of the 'liquid' and highlighted towards the ground with RMS Seafoam Blue. Jen highlighted the corks with RMS Creamy Ivory and the vial rims with RMS Leather White. The flagstones and lantern on the base were highlighted with RMS Stone Grey, and the gravelled areas base-coated with RMS Woodstain Brown.

RMS Leather White was used for a final highlight on the glass vials, metal spikes, and earring. The flagstones and lantern were highlighted with RMS Weathered Stone, then glazed randomly with Vallejo German Fieldgrey. The gravel was lightly brushed with Driftwood Brown.

Some final touches of Leather White were applied to the stones, and a last highlight of equal parts Stained Ivory and Driftwood Brown was applied to the gravel. Some areas of the gravel were glazed with Ghoul Skin for a mossy effect. Touch-ups were made in some areas with Brown Liner, a few layers of RMS Brush-on Sealer were applied, and the sides of the base were painted with Walnut Brown.

ABOVE AND RIGHT **The finished project.**

Jen Haley's finished 30mm goblin ninja project.

World War II German pilot in 1/48th scale

The popularity of aircraft modelling has 'pushed' modellers into figure painting to complement and complete their aircraft models. For aircraft modellers, the techniques employed to accentuate the details of cockpits and the weathering techniques applied to the outside of the aircraft model can be directly applicable to figures. And with the recent interest in 1/48th-scale armour, this scale is fast becoming a popular size in the figure modelling realm.

Garfield Ingram is an award-winning modeller from Toronto, Canada and is primarily a painter of 1/48th-scale aircrafts. Here he shares his approach to painting a 1/48th-scale pilot figure.

To aid in handling of the figure during the painting process, the underside of the figure's heels have been drilled with a #25 drill bit as far in as the ankle. Notice that the feet were not glued to a flat base.

Mr Surfacer 1000 primer was used on the figure to help locate flaws. The primer is always thinned with lacquer thinner and sprayed on. This allows the fine detail to remain crisp and avoids brush strokes, which will show up later in the painting stage.

A #11 blade is used for scraping away any excess flash and to sharpen up detail. The blade may 'chatter', across the surface, leaving a series of sharp lines perpendicular to the direction of scraping. These 'chatter' lines must be sanded smooth with fine sandpaper.

The first stage of painting is to coat the flesh areas. Humbrol and Model Master have standard flesh colours pre-mixed and are a good match. The flesh tone is applied with a small brush, avoiding pooling in areas such as the eyes and mouth.

A thin wash of Winsor & Newton Burnt Sienna is applied to the face and hands allowing it to flow naturally into the recesses. Once it has dried, a fine-pointed brush is lightly dampened with paint thinner and stroked on the flesh area to help blend out any sharp edges that may have resulted from the wash.

Highlights are created by taking the original flesh colour and adding white. This is applied in very limited amounts to the ridge of the nose, tops of the cheeks, chin and along the forehead. Again, when it is dry, blend the edges in with a damp brush. Sharp details such as eyebrows and lips are added.

The hair is painted as a dark brown first and a medium brown value followed by a light yellow-brown to give a dark-to-light range for the hair. The line of the cap and collar must be done very carefully, making sure that the lines are sharp and even.

Similar to the face, a range of values is blended together on the life vest to accentuate the folds and details. Brown is added to basic yellow in darker and darker stages to create the recesses of the folds. White is added to the basic yellow to create the highlights.

Pin washes of very dark brown oil paint are applied with a very fine brush to pick out deep, dark shadows of the straps and opening. The dark wash at the edges of the yellow will also provide a bit of a transition from the very light vest to the dark uniform, making it more realistic.

Humbrol #77 is applied to areas of the uniform using a small, pointed brush. The paint should be allowed to cure for up to 24 hours, as several applications of thin washes will follow to the base colour. Humbrol paints dry very flat and look like cloth fabric.

Black is not usually a good value to add to create shadows of a colour, but at this scale it should work well. There are at least two shades of dark grey, which are painted into the folds of the uniform and blended the usual way. Very dark grey or even black can be used as a fine line or wash underneath the edge of pockets and the jacket to accentuate the shadow.

White is added to the basic grey to create the first level of highlight on the tops of the folds. Take your time to blend them into the surrounding area after leaving them to dry for an hour or less. The lightest value is then added to the very tops of the folds and blended in.

The final details include adding semi-gloss black for the boots and hat brim while silver is used to pick out the details. Fortunately, in this case, the figure was made of metal and the piping lines were created by scraping away the paint with the tip of a #11 blade.

This is the completed figure from behind; it can be seen that an equal amount of time was spent on blending the colours on the back as on the front.

The completed Dartmoor figure is taken out of the vice and placed next to a 1/48th-scale Tamiya FW-190 built by George Burfield.

Large-scale figures

In the larger scales such as 120mm, 200mm, and 1/6th scale, figure painting has become very much an art form of its own, with stunning results. The quality of workmanship is easily on a par with the modelling of 54mm and 1/35th-scale historical and military figures. With a huge (and growing) community and the level of realism that can be attained by a skillful 1/6th devotee, it is unquestionable that this form of miniaturism falls well within the scope and nature of conventional modelling.

Modelling a Confederate soldier in 1/6th scale

Action Man is a 1/6th-scale (1ft tall) doll marketed as a 'movable fighting man' with 'real gripping hands and real hair', and was based on the Hasbro 1964 GI Joe figure. Over the years, the Action Man series became a very collectible piece of memorabilia and has fast become a hugely popular hobby in its own right. This new hobby – 1/6th-scale modelling – focuses primarily on the customization of commercially produced 1/6th-scale action figures along with the accessories and vehicles.

While this is a fairly new hobby, it is certainly one that should not be overlooked and much can be learned from it. A significant focus of these miniaturists is military subjects of many different eras, while others focus on science fiction, fantasy, popular culture, famous personalities or civilian topics. While many conventional modellers argue that this hobby is not actual modelling, many 1/6th enthusiasts make their own custom uniforms, weapons, helmets, equipment as well as sculpting and painting heads and custom-building scale model military vehicles and armour.

Lee Dobson is a true master in this miniature art form and shares his approach to repainting a 1/6th-scale head of a Confederate Missouri guerrilla from the American Civil War.

Choosing the right head for customizing was an important step. This commercially painted head is actor Robert Patrick from the film *Terminator II*.

Lee opted to strip the head of its paint and used Halford's brand of cellulose thinners to remove the paint. When using such materials, use protective gloves and work in a well ventilated room. An old toothbrush was used to scrub off the surface paint.

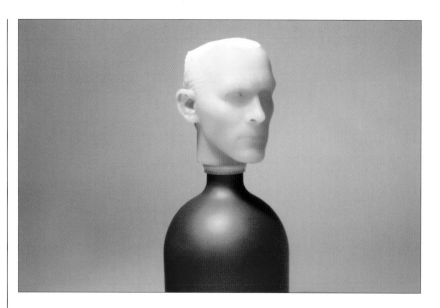

Once fully stripped, the head was washed in soap and water and temporarily glued to a handling pos

The head was covered with a beehive hat from Sideshow Toys. Fimo and Sculpey polymer clays were worked and sculpted onto the surface of the head using various-sized knitting needles; a scalpel was used to create hair.

Once baked and cooled in an oven (30 minutes), the head was primed using Matt White Halford's acrylic primer to bring out the detail of the sculpt and reveal any mistakes.

Vallejo Game colour #72003 was used for the pale flesh basecoat. The eyes were blocked using Miniature Paints #56 Cream and the beard, hair and eyebrows were painted in using Lifecolor #FS30045 French Brown.

The iris, eyelashes and nostrils were painted in with Miniature Paints #86 Umber.

The tear ducts, eyelids and mouth slit were washed in with Games Workshop Flesh Wash ink. The lips were painted in with a warm dark pink shade mixed from various Games Workshop paints. A pale green colour was mixed for the iris and painted over the Umber base, ensuring a thin outline of Umber was left around the iris.

The easiest way to paint a pupil in the eye is to dip the end of a cocktail stick/toothpick into black paint and dot the eye with it – much easier than attempting to do this with a paintbrush.

The same method was used to apply a white 'sparkle' highlight to the eyes. A small amount of gloss was added to the eyes to bring these to life.

Rowney Light Red and Raw Umber artist's oil paints were diluted with pure turpentine to make a warm, reddish wash, which was brushed all over the head, except for the eyes.

Pure Raw Umber was blended into the eye sockets and inside the ears to provide the shadows. The moustache was stippled and blended with the same, and then the whole was left to dry for a few days.

The final stage is to add tones to areas of the skin. Crimson pastel chalk was applied onto the cheeks, under the eyes, the ears and the end of the nose with a cotton swab (Q-tip) to

increase the effect of a cold winter scenario.

The hat was painted with a basecoat of Lifecolor Matt Brown, weathered with Raw Umber oil paints, earth- and sand-coloured acrylics. The hatband was painted with Miniature Paints 86 Umber, and once dry was dusted with a beige pastel chalk.

The head was mounted onto a Medicom RAH 301 body. The shirt, sack coat, 1860 Colt pistols and trousers were made by Battle Gear Toys. The clothing was weathered using watercolour paint, acrylics and pastel chalks. All of the pistols had the casting lines cleaned up and were repainted, and the metal parts were dusted with ground pencil graphite.

The completed project on a wooden base covered in wood filler with Raw Umber acrylic and some very fine grit added for texture. Suitable twigs were used as logs, and were given a green acrylic wash to depict moss. The autumn leaves were made from printer paper using a leaf-shaped punch, then painted with various brown shades of watercolour and shaped between thumb and finger.

Gallery

American Civil War 54mm metal figure by La Torre painted by Mark Bannerman in enamels (Humbrol).

Mexican Gun Fighter 54mm metal figure by Andrea Miniatures painted by Denis Allaire in oils.

93rd Sutherland Highlanders bust from Elite Miniatures, 1/10th scale in resin. Painted by Eddy Vandersteen in oils.

Geisha Girl by PiliPili painted by Le Van Quang.

'Rainy Mountain Charlie' by Poste Militaire. Metal and resin in 1/10th scale. Painted in oils by Eddy Vandersteen.

The King's Musketeer in 1/6th scale produced by PiliPili in resin and painted in oils by Eddy Vandersteen.

Geisha Girl by PiliPili painted by Le Van Quang.

German Officer by Pegaso Models in metal. Painted in oils by Eddy Vandersteen.

Landsknecht by Pagan Art in 1/10th scale, painted in oils by Eddy Vandersteen.

Exotic Lady by Pegaso Models reworked with Milliput in 1/9th scale, and painted in oils by Eddy Vandersteen.

Hawkeye Native Indian by PiliPili painted by Le Van Quang.

Yellow Moon by PiliPili painted by Le Van Quang.

ABOVE Teahouse Waitress by PiliPili painted by Le Van Quang.

BELOW A 1/16th-scale British paratrooper in Northern Ireland, by Lee Dobson.

Further reading and resources

Internet sites and discussion groups

Missing Lynx	www.missing-lynx.com
Military Modelling	www.militarymodelling.com
Planet Earth	www.planetfigure.com
Paintrix	www.paintrix-miniatures.com
Quindia wargaming	www.quindia.com

Books and magazines

Ancient and Medieval Modelling – written by Peter Armstrong (ISBN: 9781841760070).

Building and Painting Scale Figures – written by Shep Paine (ISBN: 9780890240694).

Military Modelling – high-quality monthly magazine from the United Kingdom.

Military Modelling Masterclass – written by Bill Horan (ISBN: 9781872004099).

Modelling Fallschirmjäger Figures – written by Jaume Ortiz Forns, Daniel Alfonsea (ISBN: 9781841768960).

Modelling Waffen-SS Figures – written by Calvin Tan (ISBN: 9781841768373).

Napoleonic Plastic Figure Modelling – written by Bill Ottinger (ISBN: 978-1859150191).

Terrain Modelling – written by Richard Windrow (ISBN: 9781841760629).

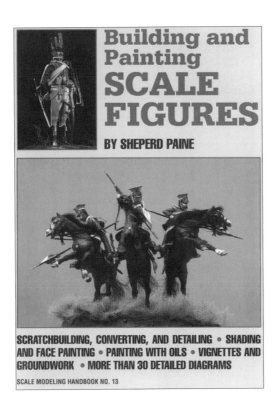

Building and Painting SCALE FIGURES

BY SHEPERD PAINE

SCRATCHBUILDING, CONVERTING, AND DETAILING • SHADING AND FACE PAINTING • PAINTING WITH OILS • VIGNETTES AND GROUNDWORK • MORE THAN 30 DETAILED DIAGRAMS

SCALE MODELING HANDBOOK NO. 13

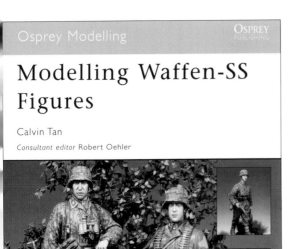

Osprey Modelling

OSPREY PUBLISHING

Modelling Waffen-SS Figures

Calvin Tan

Consultant editor Robert Oehler

NAPOLEONIC PLASTIC FIGURE MODELLING

Bill Ottinger's
HISTOREX MASTERCLASS

Windrow & Greene PUBLISHING

Manufacturers of figures

There are hundreds of manufacturers on the market of figurines of all sizes and subject matter. The following represents some of the better-known companies that offer quality products:

AIRFIX
ANDREA MINIATURES
ALPINE MINIATURES
ART GIRONA
ATHENS MINIATURES
AZIMUT
BENEITO
D.F. GRIEVE
DOG TAG
DRAGON DML
ELITE MINIATURES
HECKER & GOROS
HISTOREX
HORNET MODELS
JON SMITH MODELBAU
LATORRE FIGURES
LE CIMIER
METAL MODELS
MIG PRODUCTIONS

NEMROD
PEGASO MODELS
PHOENIX FOLIES
PILI PILI
POSTE MILITAIRE
PRESTIGE FIGURES
RESICAST
ROMEO MODELS
SHENANDOAH MINIATURES
SOLDIERS
S & T ENTERPRISES
TAMIYA
ULTRACAST
ULRICH PUCHA
VERLINDEN
WILD WEST
WARRIORS
WOLF MINIATURES
YOUNG MINIATURES

Reputable wholesalers of figurines

Red Lancers (US) – www.redlancers.com
Historex Agents (UK) – www.historexagents.com/shop/hxshop.php
Mission Models (US) – www.missionmodels.com/home.php
Hornet Hobbies (Canada) – www.hornethobbies.supersites.ca

Glossary

accelerator	A chemical used to speed up the curing time of glue.
after-market parts	Extra parts that can be bought and added to a model kit or figure, not made by the original kit manufacturer.
basecoat	The first application of paint to a figure, also known as 'undercoat'. Typically, a basecoat requires at least two applications.
blending	Blurring and softening the border between two adjacent and different colours.
capillary action	The spread of liquid into recesses and crevices on a model.
de-bonder	A chemical that dissolves glue bonds that have already dried.
dry-brushing	A technique for bringing out fine details on protruding surfaces to emphasize highlights, by dragging or lightly whisking a wide brush with very little paint across the surface of the figure.
dry-fitting	Test-fitting the join of two parts of a model without glue, to ensure that the fit is correct.
ejector marks	A slight indent or mark produced by the action of the ejector pins on the warm casting of a plastic kit as it comes out of the die.
filler	A material used for filling in gaps, seams or steps following assembly of a model.
flash	A thin boundary of ragged plastic around parts in a kit.
glazing	Similar to layering, but instead of diluting the paint, the paint is applied very sparingly and transparently over the surface so that the paint underneath is visible through the glaze, leaving almost a haze effect.
highlights and shadows	The purpose of adding highlights and shadows to a figure is to compensate for the lack of real light at a scaled size. As objects are reduced in size, they will lose their natural highlights and shadows. These need to be painted on to compensate for the lack of appropriate light at a scaled effect.
hobby knife	A sharp knife specifically for hobby use.
injection moulding	One of the main methods of producing plastic items, where polymer is injected into a mould that defines the shape of the moulded part.
layering	The application of successive light coats of a paint over a specific area, to gradually build up various tones. Layering is used when painting highlights and shadows with acrylics, because acrylics usually dry too fast for the physical wet-on-wet blending technique.
limited run	A kit that is produced in smaller quantities than more mainstream kits.
multi-media kit	One composed of plastic and resin, metal and other material parts.
outlining	The application of a dark thin line of paint that defines details such as clothing seams, pockets or flaps.
polystyrene	A thermoplastic polymer that can be moulded into different shapes at high temperatures.

priming	An initial coat of paint on a model. A coat of primer will even out the surface and give a good working base on which to apply other colours.
resin	The common name for a class of casting polymers typically made up of two parts; when blended, these two parts generate exothermic heat, causing the mixture to solidify.
scratch-building	The process of fabricating your own parts for a kit or figure from raw materials.
sink hole	A depression or hole in the surface of a plastic part.
sprue	The channels in a die through which plastic is injected into a mould, resulting (in modelling) in the frame containing all the parts of a kit.
styrene	The common name for plastic material, useful for scratch-building projects.
superdetailing	The addition of extra detail to a model.
superglue	Also known as cyanoacrylate. A modern adhesive that is highly effective for bonding almost any non-porous material, making it ideal for resin and metal parts.
thinner	A solution of water or alcohol added to paint etc. to dilute it.
toning	The application of a series of coats of very diluted paint to soften harsh contrasts. The paint has to be diluted 90 per cent with either water (for acrylics) or thinners (oils or enamels).
two-part epoxy glue	Synthesized from organic resins, this glue contains two parts that are mixed together. One part contains the glue itself, while the other part is a hardener.
two-part epoxy putty	A putty that comes in two parts which are then mixed together to make it set.
wash	A solution of heavily thinned paint applied to a model or figure to highlight important features.
vacuum-form (vacform)	A plastic manufacturing process that involves heating a plastic sheet until soft and then draping it over a mould. A vacuum is then applied, which sucks the sheet into the mould.
weathering	Recreating the effects of heavy use and of the environment on a scale model (dust, dirt, mud, wear and tear etc.)
wet-on-dry	The process of waiting until an oil or enamel colour has dried before putting down another colour – a particularly useful painting technique if you want to create sharp edges.
wet-on-wet	A technique used with oil paints and enamels. Adding wet paint to a wet layer of paint produces a soft, diffused look as the colours are mixed and blended.
white glue	A traditional adhesive made from the hides, bones or other parts of animals.

Index

References to illustrations are shown in **bold**.